WOMEN WHO KILL

WOMEN WHO KILL

A Chilling Casebook of True-Life Murders

Al Cimino

CONTENTS

INTRODUCTION

MURDER IS NOT an equal-opportunity activity. Just 30 per cent of serious violent crimes are committed by women and only four per cent of homicides. However, female perpetrators face particular opprobrium. The fondest memories of most of us are the times we spent as a child with our mothers and we believe that all women should be just as nurturing – but the women in this book are not like that.

Some murder their husbands – and sometimes, like Tillie Klimek, they make a habit of it. Others, like Tracey Connelly, kill their own children, while Enriqueta Martí, the 'Vampire of Barcelona', killed other people's children to make cosmetics and quack remedies out of them. Then there are those like Florence Ransom, who killed her rivals in love, Vera Renczi, who disposed of her many young lovers with poison, Phoolan Devi, who killed the men who had raped and humiliated her, and Rosemary West, for whom murder became the ultimate thrill in her depraved sex life.

There are no hard and fast rules about murder, except that there is often a compelling story attached to the crime. These case studies give a riveting insight into the lives and motives of women who decided to commit the ultimate transgression. They expose the shocking secrets that lurk in the hearts of those who pride themselves on being the caring sex.

These women are all the more frightening because you would not spot any of them as murderers at first sight. You might expect a male murderer to be recognizable by a scowl, a broken nose, multiple scars or an abundance of tattoos, but these women have no distinguishing features to give them away. True, when Phoolan Devi was the 'Bandit Queen' she was swathed in bandoliers and carried a Sten gun, but in later life, when she became a member of parliament, she looked like any other attractive Indian woman. It would have been hard to think that she was not entirely harmless.

Indeed, no one is safe. This is all the more disturbing as my new girlfriend has a similar psychological profile to many of these murderesses and I don't like the look of the new kitchen knives she has just bought. So if . . .

Al Cimino

CHAPTER 1

ROSEMARY WEST

IN 1995, ROSEMARY West was found guilty of committing ten murders. She claimed that her husband Fred West, who hanged himself before the trial began, had killed all of the victims on his own and she had not been involved, but the jury did not believe her.

Police find Heather's body

The couple lived in an ordinary three-storey house at 25 Cromwell Street in Gloucester in the south-west of England. On 24 February 1994, the police turned up with a warrant to dig up the back garden. The door was answered by Stephen West, the 20-year-old son of Fred and Rosemary. He was informed that the police were looking for the body of his sister Heather, who had disappeared in June 1987 at the age of 16. Stephen said his parents had told him that she had left home to work in a holiday camp in Devon and he believed that she was now living in the Midlands.

'I wanted to know the reasons why they thought Heather was buried there but they wouldn't tell me,' said Stephen, disingenuously. Among the West children there was a running joke that Heather was buried under the patio.

When Rosemary came home and saw the warrant, she became hysterical and hurled abuse at the police. She then contacted Fred, who was working on a building site about 20 minutes' drive away.

'You'd better get back home,' Rosemary told him. 'They're going to dig up the garden, looking for Heather.'

During Rosemary's interview, she told the police that Heather had been both lazy and disagreeable and they were well shot of her. Fred, in his turn, said that she was a lesbian who had become involved in drugs and, like his wife, he seemed unperturbed about her disappearance.

'Lots of girls disappear, take a different name and go into prostitution,' he said, apparently more concerned about the mess the police were making of his garden while they were raising the paving stones of his patio.

Cooking up a deal

Fred and Rosemary West stayed up all night, talking. Geoffrey Wansell, author of *An Evil Love*, a book based on 150 hours of taped interviews with Fred West, says they cooked up a deal. Rosemary was to keep silent, while Fred said 'he would "sort it out" with the police the following day, and that she had nothing to worry about as he would take all the blame'.

The next morning, Fred stepped into the police car waiting outside the house and told Detective Constable Hazel Savage, who had instigated the search: 'I killed her.'

At Gloucester Police Station, Fred told detectives how he had murdered his daughter and then buried her body, after cutting it into three pieces, adding: 'The thing I'd like to stress is that Rose knew nothing at all.'

Nevertheless, Rosemary West was arrested on suspicion of being complicit in Heather's murder and was taken to Cheltenham Police Station. When Rose was told of Fred's confession, she claimed that

Fred West promised he would 'sort it out' – if Rose kept her mouth shut about all the deaths, he would take the blame.

Fred had sent her out of the house on the day Heather disappeared. She said she had no knowledge of Heather's demise.

Twenty minutes after his confession, Fred West retracted everything he had said. He was adamant that the police could dig as much as they liked, but they would not find Heather. However, later that day the excavation team unearthed human remains. When confronted with this fact, West again confessed to killing his daughter. During an argument he had accidentally strangled her, he said, and in an effort to resuscitate her he had put her in the bathtub and dowsed her with cold water. Disturbingly, he said that to do this he had found it necessary to take her clothes off.

When the cold-water treatment did not work he had tried to put her body in the large rubbish bin, but it would not fit, so he decided to dismember the corpse. First, though, he wanted to make sure she was dead, so he strangled her with her tights. Then he cut off her head and legs.

That night, when the rest of the family was asleep, he said he buried Heather in the garden, where she had lain undiscovered for seven years. However, Professor Bernard Knight, the pathologist assigned to the case, immediately noticed that there were three leg bones among the remains the excavation team had unearthed. Clearly, there was more than one body buried in the garden at 25 Cromwell Street. Fred West was again forced to make a confession. He agreed to accompany the police back to the garden and show them where he had buried two other girls – 17-year-old Alison Chambers and 18-year-old Shirley Robinson, who had both disappeared in the late 1970s. Again, Rosemary had nothing to do with it, he claimed. He did not tell them about the six other bodies he had buried underneath the floor of the cellar and bathroom of the house, but when they were discovered he said Rosemary had nothing to do with them either.

Rosemary West's early life

Rosemary West, née Letts, was born on 29 November 1953 to a dysfunctional family. Her father, Bill Letts, was a schizophrenic who demanded total obedience from his wife and children and he was always on the lookout for reasons to beat them.

'We were not allowed to speak and play like normal children,' said Rose's brother Andrew. 'If we were noisy, he would go for us with a belt or chunk of wood.'

In the thrall of a violent husband, Rose's mother Daisy suffered from severe depression, so in 1953 she was hospitalized and given electroshock therapy. She was pregnant with Rosemary at the time and this may have affected the newborn child. In her cot Rosemary developed the habit of rocking violently – sometimes so violently that she could move her pram across the room, even when the brake was on.

A pretty child, there were rumours that she had an incestuous relationship with her father, who was known for molesting young girls. At school, Rose was teased for her chubbiness, which made her violent.

As an adolescent, Rose became sexually precocious. She would walk around the house naked, then climb into bed with her younger brother and fondle him. Outside the home she took an interest in older men, one of whom raped her. Then in 1969, the 15-year-old met 28-year-old Fred West.

Brain damage

Born in 1941 in the village of Much Marcle, some 14 miles (23 km) north-west of Gloucester, West had inherited some of his mother's less attractive features – narrow eyes and a big mouth, with a large gap between his front teeth. Scruffy and unkempt, West did not do well at school. Taunted for being a 'mummy's boy', he was a troublesome pupil and was thrashed regularly. When he left school at 15, he was practically illiterate.

At 16, West began to take an interest in girls, including his sisters. He claimed to have been introduced to sex by his mother and said that his father had committed incest with his daughters.

West claimed that his father said: 'I made you so I'm entitled to have you.' But then, he was a practised liar.

At 17, West was involved in a serious motorcycle accident, suffering a fractured skull that left him in a coma for a week. This seems to have left him with an insatiable need for sex. He then met a pretty 16-year-old girl named Catherine Bernadette Costello, nicknamed Rena. She had been a petty thief since childhood and was constantly in trouble with the police. The two misfits quickly became lovers, but the relationship was halted after a few months when Rena returned home to Scotland.

Eager for more sex, Fred became offensively forward. One night while standing on a fire escape outside a local youth club, he stuck his hand up a young woman's skirt. She reacted furiously, knocking him over the balustrade. In the fall, he banged his head again, which may well have aggravated the frontal lobe damage caused by the motorcycle accident.

Marriage to Rena Costello

Fred West then embarked on a career in petty theft. In 1961, he and a friend were caught red-handed with some stolen goods on them and were fined. His general practitioner's claim that he suffered from epileptic fits saved him from serving a jail sentence.

Soon after, he was accused of getting his 13-year-old sister Kitty pregnant but Fred was unrepentant. He did not see anything wrong in molesting underage girls, even those in his immediate family.

'Doesn't everyone do it?' he said.

His family threw him out and he went to work on building sites where, again, he was caught stealing. There were also more allegations about having sex with underage girls.

In the summer of 1962, Rena Costello returned from Scotland and took up with Fred again. They married secretly that November and moved to Scotland. Rena was pregnant by an Asian student, so when her daughter Charmaine was born in March 1963 Fred got her to write to his mother, explaining that they had adopted a mixed-race child.

West's voracious sexual appetite was by now causing problems and he preferred bondage, anal and oral sex to straightforward intercourse. Although she worked as a prostitute, Rena was not always willing to comply, but at the time West was driving an ice cream van, which gave him easy access to other young women.

In 1964, Rena gave birth to West's child, Anne-Marie, and he treated both children cruelly. The couple then met a young Scottish woman named Anne McFall. All three of them, plus Rena's two children, moved to Gloucester, where West got a job in a slaughterhouse, fuelling a morbid obsession with corpses, blood and dismemberment.

When Rena fled back to Scotland, Fred refused to let her take the two children with her. She returned to Gloucester in July 1966 to find Fred and Anne McFall living together in a caravan. Around that time there had been eight sexual assaults in the area, committed by a man who matched West's description. Increasingly worried about the safety of her children, Rena went to the police and told them that her husband was a sexual pervert and unfit to raise her daughters. This was when Constable Hazel Savage first became involved in the case.

First murder victims

By the beginning of 1967, McFall was pregnant with West's child. She put pressure on him to divorce Rena and marry her instead, but in July

West responded by killing her, dismembering her body and burying her in a field in Much Marcle. When the corpse was unearthed in 1994, the fingers and toes were missing.

After Anne McFall's disappearance, Rena moved into the caravan with West, and with his encouragement she went to work as a prostitute again. Meanwhile, he began to openly molest four-year-old Charmaine.

On 5 January 1968, pretty 15-year-old Mary Bastholm was abducted from a bus stop in Gloucester. She was never seen again and was thought to have been another of Fred West's victims. After Mary had gone missing, most girls in the area were cautious about going out, but not Rosemary Letts. On 29 November 1968, West picked up Rosemary at Cheltenham bus station.

Deaths of Rena and Charmaine

Whatever Bill Letts's shortcomings as a parent, he tried to keep his underage daughter away from West. The relationship was halted briefly when West went to prison for theft, but Rose was already pregnant with West's child. At 16, she moved into West's caravan to take care of Rena's two daughters.

In 1970, Rose gave birth to the ill-fated Heather. With Fred in jail, no money and three children to take care of, the teenage Rose found it hard to cope. She also resented having to take care of another woman's children and treated them abominably. Then in the summer of 1971 eight-year-old Charmaine went missing. Rose told Anne-Marie that their mother Rena had come to get her.

There is no doubt that Rose killed her, because Fred was in jail at the time. However, when he got out he helped Rose bury Charmaine's body under the kitchen floor of 25 Midland Road, a house in Gloucester they had recently moved into. When the corpse was found, the fingers and toes were again missing.

To earn extra money, Fred encouraged Rose to work as a prostitute. He was a voyeur and enjoyed watching her through a peephole. Although he was over-sexed, Fred would only join in if the sex involved bondage, sadism, lesbianism or vibrators.

Eventually, Rena came to look for her daughter Charmaine. Unable to get any sense out of Fred or Rose, she visited Fred's father. As a result, Fred decided to kill Rena. At the house in Midland Road, he got her drunk and strangled her. Then he dismembered her body and buried the pieces in a field near Much Marcle, not far from Anne McFall. Once more the fingers and toes were missing.

Move to Cromwell Street

Fred and Rose began employing their neighbour, 19-year-old Elizabeth Agius, as a babysitter. On more than one occasion, when the Wests returned home, Elizabeth asked them where they had been. They said they had been cruising around looking for young girls, preferably virgins. Fred explained that he had taken Rose along as they would be afraid to get into the car with him if he was alone. Elizabeth thought they were joking but then Rosemary admitted that she was a prostitute and invited Elizabeth to go to bed with her and Fred. Meanwhile, Fred propositioned her with an eye to bondage. She refused but later she was drugged. When she came to she found herself naked in bed with Fred and Rosemary.

In January 1972, Fred and Rose married at Gloucester Register Office and in June they had another daughter, Mae. They needed a bigger house to raise their growing family and so moved into 25 Cromwell Street. This house had a garage and a spacious cellar, which Fred converted into a torture chamber.

Its first inmate was his own eight-year-old daughter, Anne-Marie. Rosemary and Fred stripped her and gagged her, tying her hands behind her back, and then Rose held her down while Fred raped her.

This hurt Anne-Marie so much that she could not go to school for several days. She was warned not to tell anyone, otherwise she would be beaten, and the rapes continued.

The Cromwell Street murders

Fred and Rose continued cruising the vicinity, looking for young girls. At the end of 1972, they picked up 17-year-old Caroline Owens, whom they hired as a live-in nanny. The pair of them tried to seduce her and when she refused they stripped her and raped her. Fred threatened her with gang rape and murder if she told anyone about it, but she could not hide her bruises from her mother who called the police. In court, West was able to convince the magistrate that Caroline had consented to sex and the pair got off with a small fine. By this time Fred was 31 and Rose was 19 and pregnant for the third time.

The Wests still needed a nanny, so seamstress Lynda Gough moved into 25 Cromwell Street. Soon after, they murdered her and Fred buried her dismembered body under the floor of the garage. When Lynda's family asked what had happened to her, they were told she had moved on.

Then in August 1973 the West's first son, Stephen, was born. That November, the Wests abducted 15-year-old schoolgirl Carol Ann Cooper and took her back to Cromwell Street, where they abused her sexually. After they grew tired of this, they killed her, either suffocating or strangling her. Then her body was dismembered and buried under the house.

The following month, 21-year-old university student Lucy Partington accepted a lift from the Wests. They took her back to Cromwell Street, where they raped and tortured her for about a week and then murdered her, dismembering her body and burying it under the house.

Three more young women – 15-year-old schoolgirl Shirley Hubbard, 19-year-old Juanita Mott from Newent in Gloucestershire and 21-year-old Swiss hitch-hiker Therese Siegenthaler – ended up under the cellar floor at 25 Cromwell Street. The Wests had subjected them to extreme bondage, using plastic-covered washing lines and ropes to suspend them from one of the beams in the cellar and gagging them with tights, nylon socks and a brassiere.

In 1976, the evil pair enticed a young woman from a home for wayward girls back to Cromwell Street, where she was taken to a room in which two naked girls were being held prisoner. She was forced to watch while the two girls were tortured and then she was raped by Fred and sexually assaulted by Rose. But they did not kill her and she managed to walk free. Later, during the court case, she gave evidence as 'Miss A'.

A former prostitute, 18-year-old Shirley Robinson, then moved in as a lodger and had sex with both Rose and Fred. Rose became pregnant by one of her West Indian clients and gave birth to a daughter, Tara, in December 1977 and at the same time Shirley was pregnant with Fred's child. Rose was unhappy about this, fearing that Shirley would displace her in Fred's affections, so Shirley was murdered and buried in the back garden.

In November 1978, Rose gave birth to another daughter. This time she was Fred's child and they named her Louise. There were now six children in the household and from an early age all of them were aware of what was going on. Anne-Marie eventually fell pregnant by Fred, but it was an ectopic pregnancy so the embryo had to be aborted. She then moved in with her boyfriend, so Fred focused his sexual attentions on Heather and Mae. When Heather tried to resist, she was beaten.

In August 1979 the Wests abducted troubled 17-year-old Alison Chambers from Swansea and took her back to Cromwell Street, where she was raped and tortured before being murdered and buried in the back garden. A little less than a year later, in June 1980, Rose gave birth to Fred's second son, Barry.

Then in April 1982 Rose produced Rosemary Junior, who was not Fred's child. In July 1983 Rose bore yet another daughter, Lucyanna. It is thought that the Wests kept on carrying out sexual abductions throughout this period, but they did not bury any of the victims at 25 Cromwell Street.

In May 1987, 16-year-old Heather told a girlfriend about her father's sexual abuse, the beatings and her mother's prostitution. When Fred and Rose heard of this, they murdered Heather and buried her in the back garden, telling the other children that she had left home.

Police investigation

It was only five years later that the Wests began to run out of luck. One of the very young girls they had abducted and raped told her girlfriend what had happened and the friend went to the police. The case was assigned to Hazel Savage, now a detective constable, who knew of Fred West from 1966, when Rena had told her about his sexual perversions.

On 6 August 1992, the police arrived at 25 Cromwell Street with a search warrant. While they were looking for evidence of child abuse they found a mountain of pornography and arrested both Fred and Rosemary. Fred was charged with the rape and sodomy of a minor and Rosemary was charged with assisting him. He remained in custody while she was on bail.

DC Savage then set about interviewing the Wests' friends and family members. Anne-Marie talked openly about the abuse she had suffered at Fred's hands and she also expressed her suspicions about the fate of Charmaine. It was discovered that Rena had also gone missing. Savage checked tax and national insurance records, which showed that Heather had not been employed, drawn benefits or visited a doctor in five years.

The younger children were then taken into care. Without Fred, Rose found it hard to cope and tried to kill herself with an overdose of pills, but was saved by her son Stephen. However, the case against the Wests collapsed in court, when two key witnesses failed to testify against them.

DC Savage continued her inquiries into the whereabouts of Heather, eventually securing a warrant to dig up the Wests' garden. After the discovery of the bones, Fred was charged with the murders of Heather, Shirley Robinson and Alison Chambers. To protect Rose, Fred took full responsibility for the crimes.

The police then broadened the investigation to include the disappearance of Rena and Charmaine, along with Anne McFall. Fred West admitted murdering all three of them and with his help their bodies were found. He also sketched a map of the cellar and the bathroom, showing where six more bodies lay.

From the start, the police were convinced that Rosemary West was involved in the murders, even though she feigned shock at her husband's confessions. She played the part of the naive and innocent victim of a murderous and manipulative man. On 18 April 1994 she was charged with a sex offence and taken into custody. The murder charges would come later.

Fred West hangs himself

On 13 December 1994, Fred West was charged with 12 murders. He and Rose appeared together in court. In the dock, Fred tried to comfort Rose, but she pulled back from him. He later wrote to her, saying: 'We will always be in love . . . You will always be Mrs West, all over the world. That is important to me and to you.'

Just before noon on New Year's Day at Winson Green Prison in Birmingham, 53-year-old Fred West hanged himself with strips of bedsheet. This left Rose alone to face ten counts of murder. Clearly, though, she could not have been involved in the murder of Rena and Anne McFall, as they had been killed before she knew Fred.

Trial and conviction of Rosemary West

Her trial opened on 3 October 1995. In his closing speech, Brian Leveson QC for the prosecution maintained that Rose was the dominant force in the Wests' murderous partnership.

'The evidence that Rosemary West knew nothing is not worthy of belief,' he said.

The jury quickly came to the unanimous verdict that Rosemary West was guilty of the murders of Charmaine West, Heather West, Shirley Robinson and the other girls buried at the house. She was sentenced to life imprisonment on each of the ten counts of murder. In 1996, her appeal request was turned down. The Home Secretary then told Rosemary West that she would never be released and would have to serve a whole-life tariff.

In 2000, Rosemary West secured legal aid to launch a new appeal, maintaining that excessive publicity and chequebook journalism had prevented her from getting a fair trial. An application was made to the Criminal Cases Review Commission on 20 October 2000, but this was doomed to failure when a TV documentary revealed that Fred West had confessed to killing many more than the 12 victims he had been charged with murdering.

Then, on 22 January 2003, the BBC reported that 'the wedding between jailed serial killer Rose West and session musician Dave Glover has been called off – just days after it was announced. The pair have been writing to each other for a year, but Mr Glover is reported to have pulled out because of the publicity.' Glover, a 36-year-old bass player, had been working regularly with the band Slade for eight months, but his contract was quickly terminated.

In 2008, Rosemary West was transferred to the all-women prison at Low Newton in County Durham, where she has a private room complete with TV set, radio, CD player and her own bathroom. She listens to *The Archers* and Neil Diamond, plays Monopoly, cooks and has beauty products from Avon and trinkets from Argos delivered. Among the other inmates of her unit is Tracey Connelly, mother of Baby P, with whom she has had a lesbian affair.

Her daughter Mae believes that there could be as many as 30 more victims. She stopped any contact with her mother after she said she could come clean if she wanted to, but continued to maintain her silence. In 2018, the *Sun* newspaper reported that Rose had found religion in jail, saying that God would forgive her. She also told other inmates: 'Fred made me do it.'

CHAPTER 2

AILEEN WUORNOS

AILEEN WUORNOS NEVER made any secret of the fact that she hated men. When she hung out in The Last Resort, a Hells Angels bar in Port Orange, Florida, drinking and popping pills, she cursed all men and boasted that she would get even with this rotten masculine world.

The Hells Angels put up with her and called her Spiderwoman for the black leather outfits she wore. Just another outcast like them, she had certainly come from a tough background.

Troubled childhood

Aileen Carol Wuornos was born in Rochester, Michigan, on 29 February 1956, the second child of teenaged parents Diane Wuornos and Leo Pittman. Her first recollections were of her mother screaming while her alcoholic father dished out another brutal beating. When she was five, he abandoned his family. He was later sentenced to life imprisonment for raping a child and hanged himself in his prison cell. Her young mother, unable to stand her 'crying, unhappy babies', left Aileen and her elder brother Keith in the care of her parents, who adopted them.

Their grandparents were both alcoholics who spent little money on food, so the children went hungry. Aileen's grandfather would also beat her, forcing her to strip first. For fun, 'Lee' – as she liked to call herself – and Keith used to enjoy starting fires with lighter fuel, but at the age of six things went wrong and she suffered burns to her face, scarring her for life.

As well as doing badly at school, she also began offering sexual favours to older boys in return for a sandwich and a drink. By the time

Aileen Wuornos – her teenage dad dished out brutal beatings to her mother and hanged himself in his prison cell.

she was 12 she was prostituting herself for beer and cigarettes, before moving on to drugs. A friend of the family then raped her.

Takes to the road

Aileen became pregnant before the age of 15. Her son was born in a Detroit maternity hospital on 23 March 1971 and was given up for adoption. When her grandmother died some months later, Aileen dropped out of school. Her grandfather then killed himself and Keith turned to crime. By the age of 19, Aileen found herself all alone in the world and took to the road as a wandering prostitute, hitch-hiking from state to state.

In May 1974, at the age of 18, Aileen Wuornos – using the alias 'Sandra Kretsch' – was arrested in Colorado for disorderly conduct, drunk driving and firing a .22 pistol from a moving vehicle. She left town before her trial and returned to Michigan, where she was arrested for assault and disturbing the peace when she hurled a pool ball at a bartender. For this, and outstanding charges of driving without a licence and drinking while driving, she was fined $105.

At 20, she married 69-year-old Lewis Gratz Fell, beating him with his walking stick when he refused her constant demands for money. He took out a restraining order and filed for divorce. Then came a rare stroke of luck. When her brother Keith suddenly died from cancer in July 1976, Aileen was surprised to receive an insurance payout of $10,000, but she quickly squandered the money, buying a car which she promptly wrecked.

Back on the road, Aileen set off for Florida. She occasionally worked as a barmaid or cleaner, but her love of alcohol and drugs meant she could never hold down a job for long. With no fixed abode she hitch-hiked around the highways of Florida, sleeping outdoors on the beach or at the roadside and supporting herself with prostitution, petty crime and cheque forgery.

On 20 May 1981, she was arrested in Edgewater, Florida for the armed robbery of a convenience store. Released from prison in June 1983, she faced numerous charges – passing forged cheques, car theft and driving offences – over the next two years. On many occasions the police found a firearm in her car.

The Last Resort became more of a home to her than anywhere else, despite its collection of souvenir panties and bras on the ceiling and walls papered with centrefolds. She sometimes slept on the porch or in the so-called Japanese hanging gardens, where the Angels hung despised Japanese motorcycles from the trees, and was known to one and all as a foul-mouthed, ill-tempered drunk.

Meets Tyria Moore

In June 1986 Aileen met up with 22-year-old Tyria Moore in a gay bar in Daytona, Florida. It was a deeply romantic affair. Aileen believed Tyria would put an end to her loneliness and thought she would never abandon her in the way everyone else in her life had done. They were lovers for a year or so, but remained close companions for four years, and were regularly in trouble with the law as they drifted around Florida, living in trailer parks and seedy apartments. Most of the time, Aileen adopted the alias of 'Susan Blahovec'. She worked as a prostitute at truck stops and in bars, or thumbed lifts in pursuit of her trade. By this time she was becoming increasingly belligerent with her clients and always carried a loaded pistol in her bag.

Then in June 1990 the two women abandoned a car after being involved in an accident and their descriptions were put into the Marion County computer. They matched those of two women wanted in connection with six murders in the area. The victims were all men and their bodies had been found dumped miles from where their cars had been found. Each had been shot with a small-calibre revolver and there was a condom wrapper left on the back seat of each of their cars.

Series of murders

The first murder had taken place in 1989, when a car belonging to 51-year-old electronics repairman Richard Mallory was found abandoned on 30 November, with his wallet and its contents scattered close by. Two weeks later, his body, fully clothed, was found in the woods north-west of Daytona Beach. He had been shot three times with a .22 pistol. Then on 1 June 1990, the naked corpse of 43-year-old David Spears was found in woodland 40 miles (64 km) north of Tampa. He had been missing since 19 May and had been shot six times with a .22-calibre weapon.

Only a few days later, on 6 June, the naked body of 40-year-old Charles Carskaddon was found north of Tampa. Carskaddon had vanished on 31 May after leaving Bonneville, Missouri. He had been shot nine times with a .22 pistol and his car was discovered the following day. His personal belongings, including his .45 automatic, had been stolen. Despite the similarities in these cases, the police still refused to recognize that a serial killer was at work in Florida.

Sixty-five-year-old Peter Siems was last seen when he left home near Palm Beach on 7 June, bound for Arkansas to visit relatives. On 4 July, his car was found wrecked and abandoned, 200 miles (322 km) to the north. Witnesses to the crash were able to describe two women leaving the vehicle, one blonde and one brunette. The blond woman was bleeding from an injury and a bloody palm print was obtained from the car boot. As Siems was considerably older than the previous victims and was an evangelical missionary, it was thought unlikely that he had picked up a prostitute. It seemed more likely that he had given a lift to two apparently harmless hitch-hikers. According to leads, women answering the same description had been seen near the other crime scenes. One was stocky and the other thin, with a tattoo on her arm.

Then came 50-year-old Eugene Burress, who was reported missing from Ocala, in central Florida, on 30 July. His empty truck was found the following day. Nearly a week later, his badly decomposed but fully clothed body was discovered by picnickers in Ocala National Forest. He had been shot twice with a .22 pistol. His credit cards had been scattered around and an empty cash bag from a local bank was found at the scene.

Also missing from Ocala, on 11 September, was Dick Humphreys, a 56-year-old retired police chief from Alabama. The following day his clothed body was found, shot seven times with a .22-calibre weapon. His car was found two weeks later, some 100 miles (161 km) to the north, but it was not traced to Humphreys until 13 October, when his badge and other personal items were discovered 70 miles (113 km) to the south-east.

The corpse of 60-year-old Walter Antonio, a trucker and reserve police officer from Merritt Island, on Florida's east coast, was discovered near the north-west coast on 19 November. He was naked apart from his socks. His clothes were found later in a neighbouring county and his car was discovered back east on 24 November. He had been shot three times in the back and once in the head, and his police badge, nightstick, handcuffs, handgun and flashlight had been stolen.

Intense media pressure at last forced the police to acknowledge that these killings were related. The police published sketches of the two women seen fleeing the wreck of Peter Siems' car in the newspapers and readers phoned in with the name of Tyria Moore and her lover Lee, along with various other aliases she used.

Arrest

Over the next three weeks, searches of motel receipts uncovered the movements of 'Lee Blahovec', 'Lori Grody' and 'Cammie Greene' and fingerprint analysis identified the wanted woman as Aileen Wuornos. Meanwhile, she was raising money by pawning identifiable property stolen from her victims, leaving more telltale fingerprints.

Shortly after wrecking Peter Siems' car, Tyria left Aileen and fled to Pennsylvania. In January 1991, the police traced her there and arrested her for auto theft. Also, valuable items belonging to the victims were found in her suitcase. Tyria broke down and blamed Aileen. She had lured her into a life of crime, Tyria said, and Aileen had murdered and robbed to buy her expensive gifts.

Aileen was picked up on the porch of The Last Resort, asleep. She thought she was being arrested for a five-year-old firearms charge. While Aileen was in jail, the police got Tyria to telephone her and say she was afraid she was going to be charged with the murders.

'I'm not letting you go to jail,' Aileen replied. She then confessed to the killings, pleading that they were all done in self-defence as she feared being raped or killed. After her conviction, she admitted that this was a lie.

Dredging Rose Bay near The Last Resort, the police found a .22 weapon, along with a flashlight and a handgun belonging to Walter Antonio. Aileen's MO was straightforward. She would be hitch-hiking and her victim would stop his car to offer her a lift, or sometimes she would pretend that her car had broken down and she needed help. Either way, once in the man's car she would offer to have sex with him and then get him to drive to a deserted spot. After sex, she would then take her vengeance on all mankind by killing her victim, robbing him of his money and valuables into the bargain. Even the hardened Hells Angels were shocked when they discovered that they had been harbouring a man-slayer.

Trial and execution

Aileen Wuornos stood trial on 13 January 1992, charged with the murder of Richard Mallory. The star witness for the prosecution was Tyria Moore. As the only witness in her own defence, Wuornos took the stand and testified that she had been violently raped, sodomized,

tortured and beaten by Mallory and that she had only shot him when
he threatened to kill her. The jury did not believe her and on 27
January Wuornos was found guilty. When the jury recommended the
death penalty two days later, she cried out: 'I'm innocent! I was raped!
I hope you get raped! Scumbags of America!'

Ten months later, a TV reporter unearthed the fact that Mallory
had indeed served ten years in another state for violent rape. By then,
however, Wuornos had pleaded guilty to the killings of Spears, Burress
and Humphreys and had received the death sentence for all three. She
also offered to show the police where the body of Peter Siems was
hidden, but nothing was found at the spot she indicated and the police
believed this was merely a ruse to obtain a few days away from prison.

Despite her guilty pleas, Aileen Wuornos remained on Death Row
in Florida for ten years, consistently proclaiming her innocence and
lodging appeals. She finally went to the electric chair on 9 October
2002.

CHAPTER 3

KARLA HOMOLKA

CANADIAN SERIAL KILLER Karla Homolka claimed that her husband Paul Bernardo had beaten her and forced her to participate in his rapes and murders. Later evidence came to light that this was not true. She was a willing participant and even encouraged him. But by then she had secured a plea bargain, which enabled her to escape with a conviction for manslaughter.

Born on 4 May 1970, Karla was the eldest of the three daughters of Karel and Dorothy Homolka, who lived in St Catharines, Ontario. A bright girl, Karla did well at school but curtailed her education after taking a job in a pet store.

Meets accomplice

She met Bernardo at a conference in Toronto and after one night she knew she was going to marry him. He was 23; she was just 17. But Bernardo had had a disturbed upbringing. The man he had taken to be his father had sexually abused his sister and then his sister's daughter. Bernardo's mother was also a victim of sexual abuse and revealed to Paul that he had been born as the result of an affair.

Bernardo was a charmer who found no difficulty in getting women into bed, though he was largely interested in anal sex. He could hardly believe his luck when on their first date Karla took him into the basement of the family house, produced a pair of handcuffs and told him that she wanted to be tied up and entered from behind.

As her boyfriend, he charmed her family, who would let him stay overnight. He had a good job as an accountant with a prestigious financial firm and took her out to fancy restaurants. However, on the way from his home in Scarborough he would abduct young women – usually schoolgirls – from bus stops and rape them. To avoid capture, he would steal their IDs and tell them that he would come and find them if they reported him to the police. Karla relished the details of these rapes and it was thought that she was present on at least one occasion, filming the whole event with a video camera.

She then got a job in a veterinary clinic, where she was accused of stealing the anaesthetic ketamine, but she quickly moved on to another one, where she had access to halothane, which was used in general anaesthesia. Meanwhile, Bernardo quit his job as an accountant, finding he could make more money smuggling cigarettes.

On 9 December 1989, Bernardo proposed and the date of the wedding was set for 29 June 1991. However, their marriage prospects were threatened when the police released photographs of the Scarborough Rapist and several people identified Bernardo. He promptly bleached his hair blond. When the police interviewed him they did not believe that such a charming young man could be a vicious criminal, though his name remained on a longlist of other possible suspects. Even the blood and saliva samples he gave were filed for 25 months before being sent for analysis.

Death of sister

Karla knew that Bernardo was upset because she was not a virgin when he met her, so she decided to give him the virginity of her 15-year-old sister, Tammy-Lynn, instead. She began by breaking the blinds

In thrall to Bernardo, Homolka was quite happy to sacrifice her younger sister for sexual kicks.

in Tammy's room, so he could watch her undress, and then Karla and Bernardo had sex in Tammy's bed, with Karla pretending to be her sister. Later, she seized an opportunity to drug Tammy with valium and the couple sneaked into her room while she was unconscious. Bernardo masturbated beside Tammy's head, then tried to have sex with her, but stopped when she stirred. Instead, Karla gave him oral sex, while he fantasized that she was Tammy.

Even this was not good enough. One evening around Christmas, when Homolka's parents had gone to bed and the three of them were watching a movie, Karla slipped some sleeping pills into Tammy's drink and then sedated her with halothane. After that, she pulled down Tammy's panties so Bernardo could enter her. Between rapes, Karla would perform oral sex on both Tammy and Bernardo.

Overdosed on drugs, Tammy began to choke on her own vomit and then stopped breathing. Bernardo performed CPR but it did no good. They then called 911, but when the paramedics arrived Tammy was dead. The paramedics were surprised to learn that the blanket Tammy had vomited on was already in the washing machine, but the police decided that the 15-year-old had killed herself by drinking too much and her death was a tragic accident.

The day after Tammy's funeral, Bernardo brought a girl home and raped her in front of Karla. After he had let the victim go on the edge of town, he then had sex with Karla in front of the video camera, while she pretended to be Tammy.

Body sawn up

Once they moved into their own house, these rapes became a regular occurrence. Karla would bring home a teenage colleague from work and drug her with halothane and then they would video themselves sexually assaulting her.

On 14 June 1991, 14-year-old Leslie Mahaffy found herself locked out of her home for staying out late. Bernardo had already spotted her in the street and followed her, hoping that he could spy on her while she undressed for bed. When she asked him for a cigarette he pulled a knife, blindfolded her and drove her home, telling Karla that she was their new playmate.

Bernardo raped Leslie repeatedly while Karla was at work, then showered her ready for when she returned. Again their assaults were videotaped. At one point, Bernardo said: 'You're doing a good job, Leslie, a damned good job . . . The next two hours are going to determine what I do to you. Right now, you're scoring perfect.' Later, she was heard screaming and begging for mercy as he sodomized her with her hands bound.

During the abuse, Leslie's blindfold slipped. Fearing that she could identify them, they decided to kill her. Bernardo claimed that Homolka poisoned her with a lethal dose of halothane and Homolka said that Bernardo strangled her.

Bernardo cut up Leslie's body with a circular saw and encased the pieces in cement, depositing the blocks in a nearby lake. These were discovered by canoeists and the victim was identified from dental records as Leslie Mahaffy. But there was nothing to link her to Homolka and Bernardo, who went ahead with their wedding untroubled.

Held hostage and murdered

On 16 April 1992, the newly-weds were out on the hunt together when they spotted 14-year-old Kristen French walking home from Holy Cross Secondary School. They pulled up and Homolka got out of the car holding a map, pretending she needed directions. Bernardo then approached Kristen from behind with a knife and forced her into the car. They spent three days torturing, raping and sodomizing her – and, of course, videoing it all. Kristen had not been blindfolded throughout the whole ordeal, so it was clear they meant to kill her. Her naked body was found in a ditch with her hair shaved off and her face staved in to hamper identification.

Karla accuses Bernardo

Meanwhile, Karla played Kristen whenever they had sex, dressing up in an outfit that looked like her school uniform.

'Hellmaster,' she said one night. 'I'm your Holy Cross sex slave.'

'Are you ready to get f****d up the ass?' he asked.

'Yes, master,' she said. 'All the girls at Holy Cross want to get f****d up the ass by you.'

On another occasion during sex, Bernardo put on a tape where he was raping Tammy. This scene was taped too, with Homolka fondling her husband's penis, which she called Snuggles, and performing fellatio, stopping every now and then to talk about her dead sister.

'I loved it when you f****d my little sister,' she said. 'I loved it when you f****d Tammy. I loved it when you took her virginity. You're the king. I love licking your ass, Paul. I'll bet Tammy would have loved to lick your ass. I loved it when you shoved Snuggles up her ass.'

Kristen's parents called the police soon after she failed to return home from school and the abduction had been seen by several witnesses. But detectives still did not link the crime to Homolka and Bernardo, who had been interviewed by the police several times in connection with the death of Tammy-Lynn. Bernardo was also a suspect in the Scarborough Rapist case and had been reported several times for stalking. Nevertheless, he continued bringing victims home to be drugged and sexually abused, clearly with Homolka's connivance and consent.

But Bernardo overstepped the mark when he began making sexual advances to mutual friends, even climbing into bed naked with a house guest. There were frequent rows and one day Karla turned up to work with two black eyes and other injuries. Co-workers called her mother, who went to collect her, but Karla had already gone home on her own. Her mother called Karla's home and spoke to Karla and Bernardo, who both assured her that everything was okay, but when she visited the next day it was clear that Karla had been beaten again. She persuaded Karla to leave her husband and after leaving the house Karla told her mother that Bernardo had killed Tammy-Lynn.

Homolka and Bernardo sentenced

Once Karla had been treated in the emergency room of St Catharines General Hospital, the police arrested Bernardo for beating his wife. Finally, the DNA blood and saliva he had given over two years earlier was matched to that of the Scarborough Rapist.

Karla also told relatives that Bernardo had killed Kristen French and Leslie Mahaffy. She then hired a lawyer, seeking immunity from prosecution. The Crown Prosecutor refused, but said he could offer a deal which would guarantee her a reduced sentence if she co-operated.

Bernardo was arrested for the Scarborough rapes and the murders of the two girls and then detectives began going through the video they found at the Bernardos' house. It soon became clear that Karla was not the abused wife she made herself out to be and that she had not been forced into depravity by a brutal husband. Instead, she was enjoying herself.

Sentencing her, the judge said: 'No sentence I can impose would adequately reflect the revulsion of the community at the death of those young girls, who lived lives beyond reproach. I understand the outrage the community feels, and rightly so.'

Nevertheless, it had been agreed that she would serve two ten-year sentences concurrently for the manslaughter of Kristen French and Leslie Mahaffy, along with two years for her involvement in the rape and murder of her sister. This was dubbed the 'deal with the devil' by the media.

In return, Karla testified against her husband, saying that she had agreed to give her sister Tammy's virginity to him as a 'Christmas present'. But during various sexual acts she had encouraged him by saying 'You're the master' and 'You are the king'. Bernardo and Homolka were quickly characterized as the 'Ken and Barbie' killers.

Karla was subjected to a searching cross-examination after videos were shown of her having oral sex with an unconscious woman and aiding her husband to deflower teenage virgins. She showed no remorse over the death of her sister Tammy or the murders of Kristen French and Leslie Mahaffy. Instead, blaming everything on her husband, she told the court: 'I think he's a monster.'

Homolka spent 16 days on the witness stand. Despite evidence of the beatings she had received, there was little sympathy for her in the courtroom. One man shouted out that she was a murderer before she was escorted back to the safety of her cell.

Release of Homolka

While Bernardo admitted raping and torturing Kristen French and Leslie Mahaffy, he maintained that Homolka actually killed them. He was sentenced to life imprisonment and later on he was classified as a dangerous offender, so he would never be eligible for parole. Homolka served her entire 12-year sentence without even applying for parole. In jail she had a lesbian affair with Lynda Véronneau, who wrote a book about it, and began a relationship with a male prisoner, Jean-Paul Gerbet. After her release, Homolka was forbidden to communicate with Gerbet, who was due to be deported to France on completion of his sentence anyway.

Homolka then changed her name and moved to Francophone Canada, where she thought she was less likely to be recognized, telling Canadian TV: 'I am unable to forgive myself . . . what I did was terrible.' Explaining her move to Quebec, she told the interviewer: 'I don't want to be hunted down . . . I don't want people to think I am dangerous.'

Homolka gave birth to a son before moving on to Guadeloupe, where she was found in 2012 living with her new husband, the brother of her lawyer, and three children.

CHAPTER 4

KATHERINE KNIGHT

KATHERINE KNIGHT WAS the first woman in Australia to be sentenced to life imprisonment without the possibility of parole. After having sex with her common-law husband, she stabbed him 37 times. When sentencing her, the judge said: 'The last minutes of his life must have been a time of abject terror for him as they were a time of utter enjoyment for her . . . she has not expressed any contrition or remorse and if released she poses a serious threat to the security of society.'

She claimed she could not remember killing him, but after the act she had expertly skinned his corpse, chopped off his head and boiled it and served up slices of his buttocks with vegetables for his children to eat. It was also clear that she had planned the event. She bought a sexy black nightie for the initial seduction, sharpened her butcher's knives and had the cooking pots ready.

Born in 1955 in Aberdeen, New South Wales, she was the daughter of a violent alcoholic who raped her mother up to ten times a day. Katherine was also sexually abused as a child, though not by her father. On top of that, the family had Aboriginal blood and there was a great deal of racism in the area at the time.

At the age of 16, she went to work in an abattoir. It was her dream job. Colleagues remember that she was particularly adept at beheading pigs and had exhibited a perverse fascination with the front end of the production line, where the animals' throats were cut. She was so proud of her professional abilities that wherever she lived she kept her razor-sharp boning knives hanging above her bed.

'She'll . . . kill you'

In 1973, she met 22-year-old truck driver David Kellett and they married the following year. Turning up at the ceremony on Knight's motorbike, Kellett, drunk on the pillion, received some advice from his bride's mother: 'The old girl said to me to watch out. "You better watch this one or she'll f***ing kill you. Stir her up the wrong way or do the wrong thing and you're f***ed, don't ever think of playing up on her, she'll f***in' kill you." And that was her mother talking!'

True to form, Knight tried to strangle him on her wedding night, because she was not satisfied with his sexual performance – he had only made love to her three times. On another occasion, she smashed him in the face with a hot iron when he came home with a six-pack of beer. Then one morning he awoke to find her sitting on his chest while holding a knife to his throat.

'You see how easy it is,' she said. 'Is it true that drivers have different women in every town?'

After another violent outburst Kellett fled, fearing for his life. Knight then left their two-month-old daughter on the railway tracks when a train was due – the child was rescued in the nick of time by a local man. Later she was arrested for swinging an axe at passers-by. She also stabbed a policeman, but somehow escaped without charge. Instead, she was taken to hospital, where she was diagnosed with post-natal depression and released. When she found out where her husband was, she slashed a woman driver's face and demanded that she take her to him. The woman escaped, but Knight then took a child hostage and was admitted to a psychiatric hospital in Morisset, New South Wales.

With Knight under medication, the couple were reunited and moved to Queensland together, where she got a job in another meat factory. She continued the violent abuse of her husband but nevertheless they had another child. Then in 1984 they split. With their two children and all of Kellett's possessions she moved back to Aberdeen and the abattoir there, but soon lost her job due to the back strain caused by constant bending.

Restraining order

In 1986 she took up with David Saunders, another drunk, but when they moved in together the relationship grew increasingly violent. He complained that she cut up his clothes, smashed up his car, stabbed him with a pair of scissors, knocked him unconscious with a frying pan and cut the throat of his eight-week-old puppy to intimidate him. Even so, he gave her a third child.

He then put down a deposit on a small house in Aberdeen, which she paid off with her workers' compensation. She decorated the walls with cowhides, the horns of steers and water buffalo, old-fashioned fur wraps, cow and sheep skulls and deer's antlers. There was also a stuffed peacock, a baby deer and a collection of violent horror videos.

The domestic violence continued and eventually Saunders could take no more, so he fled and went into hiding. When he returned to see his daughter some months later, he discovered that Knight had reported him to the police and had taken out a restraining order to keep him away from her and the children.

Partner served up for dinner

Knight then took up with 43-year-old John Chillingworth, who also worked at the Aberdeen meat works, and they had a son. The children were now lodged with her parents. As usual, her relationship with Chillingworth turned violent. She smashed his glasses and his false teeth.

In 1994, she dropped Chillingworth for father-of-three John Price, with whom she had been having an affair. Price's wife had left him some time before, taking their youngest child with her, and Knight moved into his large brick-built bungalow on St Andrews

Knight with John Price: he was a bit of a larrikin but never missed a day's work; she loved her work in slaughterhouses and was particularly adept at beheading pigs.

Street, where he lived with his two teenaged children, Becky and John. As before, the relationship was loving at first and then came accusations of infidelity – and with them violence.

Price was a bit of a larrikin but he was a good worker and never missed a day, so when he did not turn up for work on 1 March 2000 his boss called the police. The previous Tuesday, Price had told him that Katherine had gone berserk and grabbed a kitchen knife. That night, he had woken to see her standing at the end of the bed brandishing the blade. He wanted to split from her but first she wanted him to give her his St Andrews Street home. The following day, he took out a court order to keep her away from him and his house.

But she was not to be stopped. On the evening of 29 February she took her kids to dinner, which was unusual, telling them: 'I want it to be special.'

Sensing something was wrong, her daughter Natasha said: 'I hope you are not going to kill Pricey and yourself.'

Later she went back to St Andrews Street. Arriving at around 11 p.m., she had a shower before donning the black nightie and joining Price in bed. She recalled having 'pleasurable sex' with Price before stabbing him. Bloodstains showed that he managed to get to the front door before she dragged him back. He died in the hallway after a frenzy of stab wounds had punctured all of his major organs.

After expertly skinning him, she hung his near-complete pelt in a doorway and then sliced up his flesh and prepared a grisly meal for his children. This was served up on plates accompanied by makeshift place cards. Next, she wrote a series of vindictive and barely literate notes, baselessly accusing Price of sexually abusing her daughter and his son. After that, she had a cup of coffee and a cigarette and then she took A$1,000 (£534/$709) from Price's account at a nearby ATM.

As well as Price's boss, a neighbour also alerted the police, who visited the St Andrews Street address. The police report said:

Police were contacted and attended about 8 a.m. The police
at the scene forced entry to the house through the rear door.
Upon entry the police located the victim's exterior layers of
skin hanging from a hook in a doorway arch into the lounge
room. They then located the victim's decapitated remains
on the lounge room floor near a small foyer leading to the
front door.

A further search of the house by police resulted in
them locating Katherine Knight who was snoring loudly
in a comatose condition on a double bed at the end of the
house. She was removed from the house immediately by
police and later conveyed to hospital by ambulance.

On the table were empty boxes of various tablets. Knight appeared to
have been trying to commit suicide, or perhaps was faking it.

A crime-scene officer said:

I remember walking down the hallway and at about shoulder
height there were all these blood splatter marks on the
walls. To me, it's indicative of each attack . . . He's absolutely
fighting for his life. The bloke's just had a bonk in the bed
when he wakes up, then stab, stab, stab. He's getting up,
there is arterial spurting on the robe and the bed, and on
the doorway there's a bloodied handprint or swipe on the
western side of the door near the dressing table, and blood
around the light switch. It looks like he's tried to turn the
light switch on. And then all down the hallway they're
[bloody handprints] everywhere. And he's almost made it,
he's opened the front door, the screen door is shut, there
is blood staining, trajectory again, flicking out across the

front door, he's almost made it . . . but he wouldn't have survived. He would have been absolutely horrified, terrified – probably terrified more than horrified – trying to get out and all the time being stabbed.

A report by Detective Senior Constable Peter Muscio said:

My attention was drawn to a piece of cooked meat on the rear lawn in front of the white Ford sedan. I made an examination of this piece of meat and collected it for further testing. . . .

I walked in through the rear door and into the kitchen. Once inside the kitchen I saw a large section of what appeared to be human skin hanging from the top architrave of the doorway leading into the lounge room. This piece of skin extended from the top of the doorway right to the floor and appeared to be an entire human skin. Looking through this doorway into the lounge room I could see a headless and skinless human body. I walked east along the hallway and looked into the entry foyer and saw an extreme amount of blood pooled on the floor. There was also a large amount of blood smearing over the eastern wall of the entry. . . .

In the kitchen he found:

Just to the right or northern side of the cook top I saw two prepared meals. Each of the meals consisted of two pieces of cooked meat, baked potato, baked pumpkin, zucchini, cabbage, yellow squash and gravy. Underneath each of the meals was a torn section of kitchen paper with a name written on it. The word 'Beaky' was written in blue ink pen on one of the pieces while the word 'Jonathon' was on the other. The

pieces of meat that appeared on the plates were similar to the
piece I collected from the rear lawn. . . .

During questioning, Knight said she had no recollection of what had
happened that night, beyond having sex. She recalled Price getting up
to go to the bathroom and then returning to their bed. After that, she
assumed she had gone to sleep. While being held in the psychiatric
wing of Maitland District Hospital, she was charged with murder.
Although parts of Price's body were unaccounted for, she was not
charged with cannibalism, though it was thought that she may have
eaten some pieces of tissue and blocked it from her mind. The pots
were still warm when the police arrived, so the cooking had been done
early in the morning. It was thought that the pieces of flesh found in
the back garden were bits she had tried to eat, but rejected.

At the trial, she initially pleaded not guilty but changed her plea
to guilty before the jury was empanelled. No reason for her change of
heart was given. During testimony from the pathologist, she became
hysterical when the state of the corpse was described, but showed
no remorse. She was judged to be sane and was sentenced to life
imprisonment with a whole-life tariff. Her file was stamped: 'Never
to be released.'

Knight's appeal against the sentence was dismissed and in
Mulawa Women's Correctional Centre she worked as a cleaner in
the governor's office. Although she was a good cook, it was thought
unlikely she would ever get a job in the kitchen.

CHAPTER 5

HEATHER STEPHENSON-SNELL

EARLY IN 2002 Adrian Sinclair answered an ad for a dog-sitter in the *Big Issue* magazine. It had been placed by 44-year-old Heather Stephenson-Snell, a psychotherapist. She had two Rottweilers and he was to take care of them while she attended to her patients, whom she treated at her home surgery in Crombie Avenue, York in the north of England.

Sinclair badly needed the work. He had taken a series of jobs, including being a stripper – something he had not enjoyed – and had also appeared in porn videos, but now he intended to embark on a career as a writer. Heather had similar ambitions and they soon became lovers. But Stephenson-Snell was not a straightforward person. In her teens and 20s she had been in trouble with the police for a series of offences, including petty theft and criminal damage. This had only ended when, at the age of 30, she became a mature student at York University, studying psychology.

However, she still had a wild side. She had joined an all-women bikers club affiliated to the Hells Angels and in her garage she had a den she called the Orange Pit, where she held drink and drugs parties for the members. Often drunk and high on cocaine, she started to tell Adrian increasingly strange stories. She boasted of attacking people who had crossed her and showed him her collection of guns and machetes.

'I thought it was all for show,' Sinclair said. 'Her claims were so outrageous, I thought it was bravado.'

Stalks former lover

After only a few weeks, Heather announced that she was going on a three-month writers' course in New York and wanted Adrian to move out. While she was away, he found a flat to rent in Radcliffe, on the outskirts of Manchester. Inexplicably, this annoyed Heather. Acting like a jilted lover, she began sending sexually explicit messages to Sinclair. This got worse when she discovered that he had taken up with a new woman, Diane Lomax, a divorced mother of three. Heather began calling his family and friends, claiming to be the injured party, and her sexually provocative messages to Adrian turned into outright threats.

'I'd had my address book stolen. It must have been her and she started ringing my friends and relatives,' Sinclair said. 'She could be very charming, so when she told my sisters she was in love with me they believed her. Even when I got a new flat, letters started arriving there. When I got a mobile, she started calling that. I didn't know where to turn . . . I couldn't see the police taking this very seriously, a woman pestering me from New York.'

When she returned from New York, she turned into a stalker. Diane was called a 'filthy prostitute and slag' and her house was dubbed the 'HIV factory'. In an effort to calm things down, Sinclair visited Stephenson-Snell in Crombie Avenue. They ended up having sex, which only made things worse.

Campaign of harassment

Stephenson-Snell then began a campaign of harassment, calling Adrian and Diane as often as ten times a day. She sent a card with a

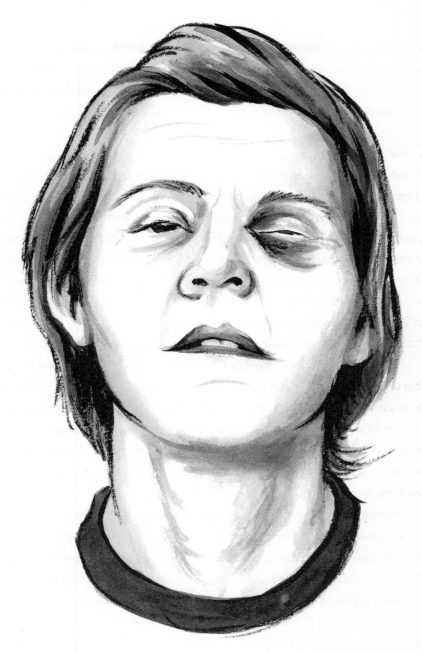

Stephenson-Snell had a wild side and joined an all-women bikers club affiliated to the Hells Angels.

picture of Adrian kissing a woman – with the woman's face scratched out – and she threatened to cut Diane's breasts off. More chillingly, she sent photographs of Diane with her children. Stephenson-Snell had been following and photographing them. She then threatened to firebomb their home.

In an effort to escape, Adrian and Diane moved to Huddersfield, 30 miles (48 km) away. While they were unpacking, the phone rang.

'It was Heather,' Sinclair said. 'She asked me what the weather was like in Huddersfield. She knew where I was. This was meant to be our new start. We had no choice but to move again.'

Adrian and Diane moved back to Radcliffe, but things got no better.

'I would stay awake all night,' said Sinclair. 'I expected her to turn up and carry out her threats any minute.'

Stephenson-Snell then called social services, anonymously alleging that Diane was abusing her children. The council was duty-bound to investigate, even though the allegations proved baseless. She also reported Ms Lomax for benefit fraud. Adrian and Diane reported her to the police but all they could suggest was that they kept a log of the harassment.

'They said they couldn't do anything because there was no evidence,' Sinclair claimed. 'Until she actually did something to me, it was no use. I felt like we weren't being believed.'

Heather then told Sinclair that through the Hells Angels she had put a £50,000 ($66,000) bounty on his head. All this had a deleterious effect on Adrian and Diane's relationship.

'We had been determined she wouldn't split us up,' said Sinclair, 'but it was too much. She was finding me whatever I did – it got to the stage where I didn't know who to trust.'

Her harassment had its effect. Although Diane and Adrian kept on seeing each other, he moved out.

'I was scared of getting involved in case Heather targeted Diane and her children too,' he said. 'I told Diane it was best for us to stay friends until all this had blown over.'

This seemed to bring Stephenson-Snell's stalking campaign to a halt. In fact, it was only moving into a new, murderous phase.

Murder plans

While Stephenson-Snell had boasted to Sinclair that she could use the guns in her weapons collection, she signed up for a course of clay-pigeon shooting at the North of England Activity Centre. At home, she used a card index system to plan the murder of Diane Lomax and the framing of Adrian Sinclair. She was going to buy a second-hand Ford Escort as a getaway car and worked out how to dispose of it. Everything was meticulously planned, right down to what she should wear. For example, her notes said she should not wear white shoes as they would show the blood. As it was, she wore trainers two sizes too big, so the size of her feet could not be used to help identify her. She also wore several layers of clothing to make her look bigger, some of which were those Adrian had left behind. The hope was that she would be mistaken for a man – if not Sinclair himself.

The attack was to take place on Halloween, so she took with her a ghostly white sheet and a 'Scream' mask when she climbed into her Ford Escort to begin the 73-mile (117-km) journey from York to Manchester. She also had with her a sawn-off shotgun, adapted so that it could hang under her spectral robe and be fired by pulling a strap.

Shoots the wrong person

Stephenson-Snell arrived at Diane Lomax's house in Holland Street, Manchester at around 12.30 on the morning of 1 November 2003. Adrian was not staying there that night, but Stephenson-Snell donned her disguise and began to hammer on the door. This woke Bob Wilkie, a 43-year-old former Royal Marine commando who was asleep next door in the house of his fiancée, 40-year-old Debbie O'Brien. Her two children from a former marriage were also there.

He went downstairs in his boxer shorts to tell whoever it was to keep the noise down, as people were trying to sleep. However, the house had no front garden or gate so when he walked through the front door he stepped straight out on to the pavement. The masked figure turned towards him and he demanded to know what they were playing at.

'Mind your own business,' said the masked figure, who then told him to get back inside.

Bob was not a man to be intimidated. He wanted to see who was confronting him so he stepped forward and pulled off the mask. A nearby CCTV camera picked up the blast of a shotgun and Bob fell backwards, hitting the ground. He had been shot in the abdomen. Women could be heard screaming and a neighbour called an ambulance, but nothing could be done. Bob Wilkie was dead.

The mysterious masked figure then disappeared, but an hour later traffic cops spotted a red G-registered Ford Escort on the M62 trans-Pennine motorway. At first they thought the driver had been drinking as the car was moving conspicuously slowly, so they pulled it over on to the hard shoulder.

Apprehended by the police

When the officer knocked on the side window, the driver, a woman, wound it down. She was not drunk but she had fresh bruising around her left eye and on her left cheek. Otherwise, she seemed to be a respectable middle-aged woman. However, she gave a name that turned out to be false.

The officer then spotted something suspicious in the footwell of the back seat and asked her to get out of the car. When he investigated, he found a white sheet stained with blood and under it he discovered a shotgun. The woman was arrested for possession of a firearm and a double-bladed knife was also found in the waistband of her suit. It soon became clear that the recoil of the shotgun had caused the butt to hit her in the face, causing the bruising.

At the police station, she constantly changed her story but nevertheless the investigation proved simple. The car had been bought recently and was registered to Ms Heather Stephenson-Snell, whose address was 137 Crombie Avenue, York. During a routine search of the property, the police found the card index system that contained the murder plans – though the target had been Diane Lomax, not Bob Wilkie.

Stephenson-Snell was then charged with the murder of Bob Wilkie and the attempted murder of Diane Lomax. The prosecutor Charles Chruszcz said: 'You were in a quite homicidal frame of mind and you had gone there to use that gun. You always intended that the gun was going to be discharged and Mr Wilkie just got in the way. He paid a terrible price for being in the wrong place at the wrong time.'

Trial and sentence

Sentencing her to life imprisonment with a minimum of 22 years for murder, Mr Justice Waverley said: 'Through an obsession with Adrian Sinclair you took the life of Robert Wilkie. As the jury have found, you deliberately fired the gun at him when he had unmasked you. . . . The plans you made were breathtaking. You planned your escape meticulously.'

The eight-year sentence for attempted murder would be served concurrently.

The judge added: 'This crime was born of obsessional behaviour. Your lies were shameless and you have shown absolutely no hint of remorse.'

Stephenson-Snell had claimed that she and Sinclair were never lovers and that he had raped her. A pathological liar, she even claimed that her father, a soldier, was a spy and helped write the cult novel *The Wicker Man*.

It transpired that Stephenson-Snell had another plan to kill Diane Lomax. In the search of her house, the police found a parcel addressed to Diane Lomax at 59 Holland Street, Radcliffe, though it had been date-stamped 28 November 2002. On the side, in Stephenson-Snell's handwriting, was the name of the 'sender': 'Adrian Sinclair, another planet, another galaxy.'

Apparently, it was a ruse to get Diane to open her front door. It was supposed to have contained a camcorder, but only shredded paper was found inside. With it was an invoice book with a request for the recipient to sign. Detective Superintendent Simon Barraclough described Stephenson-Snell as a 'jealous woman who went out on Halloween intent on causing pain and suffering'. He also said that she 'told a series of continued and sustained lies while she was in police custody and during the course of her trial'.

'She's one of the most peculiar individuals I've ever dealt with,' he added. 'A very dangerous woman has been removed from the streets.'

Unceasing nightmare

The following Halloween Adrian Sinclair was beaten up by a gang of thugs who said: 'This is for Heather.' He believed that his former lover was responsible and was still controlling her biker gang from inside jail. Talking to the *Sunday Mirror*, he said:

What has happened sounds like something from a Halloween horror movie and I wish it was but it's real life. This woman set out to destroy my life and to kill the person closest to me – she nearly succeeded. One man has already died and I'm scared I'll be next. My Halloween nightmare isn't over yet. I just wish I'd never met her. I hate this time of year, it brings all the awful memories flooding back. I can't even walk into a shop without freaking out when I see Halloween masks. And I can't leave the house on the night itself because I'm just too terrified. My own Halloween ghosts are all too real.

In the end, Stephenson-Snell got her way. Diane and Adrian split up for good.

'I want her to be free from all this to get on with her own life,' Sinclair told the newspaper. 'So I suppose Heather got what she wanted in the end. She did manage to break us up. But it's more than that – because of her obsession an innocent man, Diane's neighbour, is dead. In the name of love, she did all this. It just doesn't make sense.'

He reported his Halloween beating to the police but said they took no action.

Nevertheless, Stephenson-Snell continued to affect his life. In 2005 he said:

I still get flashbacks, I still have nightmares. I lost three stone and was on anti-depressants. At this time of year anything can set me off. I don't sleep at nights and wherever I go, whatever I do in life, I'll always be looking over my shoulder. I'll never underestimate Heather. Even now she's behind bars, because there are people who will do her dirty work for her – and if that means getting me, they will. But she won't win. I can't let her win. I've got to keep going.

CHAPTER 6

JEANNE WEBER

THE NEIGHBOURHOOD OF Goutte d'Or – Drop of Gold – in Paris was described by novelist Émile Zola as the 'dark theatre of sordid destinies'. Home to prostitutes and Apaches (bands of criminals), its reputation was not helped by serial child killer Jeanne Weber. Despite being dubbed 'The Ogress of the Goutte d'Or' by the press, she was repeatedly given the benefit of the doubt by credulous family members, employers, doctors and lawyers, which allowed her to kill and kill again. She strangled at least ten children – including three of her own – and maybe as many as 20.

Born Jeanne Marie Moulinet in the Breton fishing village of Paimpol on 2 October 1874, she cared for her younger brothers and sisters until she left home. According to her father, a fisherman from Iceland, she was very gentle with them. He also said that she was a good child who never gave her parents any trouble.

The family was poor and Jeanne was not very successful at school, so when she was 14 her parents gave her 25 francs – their entire savings – to go to Paris, which would relieve the family of one mouth to feed. She took various jobs, including working as a nanny to the five children of an architect living in Avenue de Clichy.

Deaths blamed on alcoholism

In La Chapelle, a district bordering the Goutte d'Or, she met her future husband, Jean Weber, a borderline alcoholic who worked as a timekeeper for a transport company. They married there on 2 June 1894. Her parents, now farmers in the Côtes-du-Nord (later Côtes-d'Armor), did not attend the wedding. Jeanne was pregnant at the time and their first child, Marcel Jean, was born five months later on 4 November. However, the baby died on 20 January 1895, aged almost three months. This was ascribed to husband Jean's drinking, which was thought at the time to have an adverse effect on any offspring. Jeanne was soon drinking heavily too.

A second son, Marcel Charles, was born on 9 January 1898 and a daughter, Juliette, came into the world on 3 January 1900. Juliette died on 22 January 1901, the cause of death being given as pneumonia. Again it was assumed that the children of alcoholics would have unhealthy children, though Jeanne nevertheless sought consolation in the bottle.

Deadly babysitter

Their fortunes failing, the Webers then moved from La Chapelle to the Goutte d'Or, a downmarket area on the other side of the Northern Railroad tracks, where Jeanne sought work in childcare. She was soon looking after the infant Lucie, daughter of widower Alphonse Alexandre. The child fell ill while her father was out on Christmas Day 1902 and she died soon after he returned at 4 p.m. Again, the cause of death was given as pneumonia.

Then early in 1903 she went to work as a nanny for the Poyata family, who ran a dairy in the nearby Clignacourt district. One day she was found squeezing the lifeless body of three-year-old Marcelle Poyata and once again the death was ascribed to pneumonia. A few

Le Petit Journal

Le Petit Journal
CHAQUE JOUR—6 PAGES—5 CENTIMES
Administration : 61, rue Lafayette

Le Supplément illustré
CHAQUE SEMAINE 5 CENTIMES

SUPPLÉMENT ILLUSTRÉ 5 Centimes

Le Petit Journal Militaire, Maritime, Colonial..... 10 cent.
Le Petit Journal agricole, 5 cent. ‡ La Mode du Petit Journal, 10 cent.
Le Petit Journal illustré de La Jeunesse..... 10 cent.
On s'abonne sans frais dans tous les bureaux de poste

ABONNEMENTS

SIX MOIS   UN AN
SEINE ET SEINE-ET-OISE 2 fr. 3 fr. 50
DÉPARTEMENTS............ 2 fr. 4 fr. »
ÉTRANGER............... 2 50 5 fr. »

Les manuscrits ne sont pas rendus

Dix-huitième année   DIMANCHE 12 MAI 1907   Numéro 860

L' « OGRESSE » JEANNE WEBER
Crime ou fatalité ?

In 19th-century Paris, you didn't need qualifications or clearance to look after other people's children, which served Jeanne Weber well.

days later, Jeanne returned to the Poyata household, but immediately Marcelle's four-year-old brother Jacques took fright and ran away.

Jean Weber's family still lived in La Chapelle. On 2 March 1905 his sister-in-law Blanche wanted to do the laundry in a nearby public washhouse, so she left two-year-old Suzanne and 18-month-old Georgette, her daughters by Jean's brother Pierre, in the care of Jeanne. Soon a neighbour came to the washhouse to tell Blanche that Georgette was ill with convulsions. She rushed home to find the child lying red-faced on the bed and breathing with difficulty, while Jeanne had her hand on the infant's chest. However, when Blanche took hold of the child she was soon smiling again.

Blanche then returned to finish the laundry, leaving the children in Jeanne's care once more. When she returned, Georgette was dead. Madame Pouche, a neighbour, pointed out black and blue marks around the child's neck but, perhaps out of family loyalty, Pierre Weber chose to ignore them.

Nine days later, Jeanne was asked to look after Suzanne. When her parents returned, the child was dead and again there were bruises around her neck. The doctor informed the police, but they took no action and the two-year-old was buried without further ado.

On 26 March, Jeanne arrived unannounced at the house of her brother-in-law Léon Weber and helped herself to breakfast. As it happened, his wife Marie wanted to go out, so she asked Jeanne to babysit her seven-month-old daughter Germaine. Half an hour after Marie left the apartment, Germaine's grandmother, who lived downstairs, heard the child cry out.

She went upstairs to find the infant red-faced and breathing heavily. When she took Germaine from Jeanne, the child soon calmed and began breathing normally.

After the grandmother had returned to her flat, she heard Germaine cry out again.

Quickly returning to Léon and Marie's apartment, she found the child choking. However, when Jeanne left, leaving the infant with her grandmother, she soon revived. But Jeanne returned the following day and Germaine's parents blithely left the child in her care again. She was dead when they returned and the cause of death was given as diphtheria.

Marks around victim's neck

Three days later, on 29 March, while Germaine was being buried, Jeanne's son Marcel, now seven, died after suffering convulsions. Once more the death was ascribed to diphtheria, but doctors could not explain the marks around his neck. In less than a month, four Weber children had died. In each case, they had been left alone with Jeanne Weber and on every occasion she had been found holding the dead child in a state of evident excitement, but still no one suspected that she might be to blame.

On 5 April, the wife of Charles Weber arrived from Charenton, together with her 11-month-old son Maurice. Jeanne had lunch with her and Blanche at Pierre's house and afterwards Jeanne sent her sisters-in-law out on errands, leaving her alone with Maurice. However, the child's mother returned prematurely to find Jeanne hugging the child to her, suffocating him. Wresting him from her arms, Madame Charles Weber yelled: 'You wretch! You have strangled my son!'

She rushed him to Bretonneau Hospital, where doctors revived him, and after a night of intensive care Maurice recovered. A medical student then noticed the marks around his neck and concluded that an attempt had been made to strangle the child.

Acquitted of murder

On 8 April 1905, Charles Weber and his wife filed a complaint accusing Jeanne Weber of the attempted murder of their son Maurice. Pierre

Weber followed them with a complaint about the suspicious deaths of his daughters Suzanne and Georgette, also reporting his suspicions about the deaths of his niece and nephew, Juliette and Marcel Weber. Then Léon Weber and his wife made a complaint about the death of Germaine. The deaths of Lucie Alexandre and Marcelle Poyata also featured in the investigation.

Jeanne Weber was called in for questioning but she denied everything and claimed to be the victim of 'slanderers and infamous rascals'. She was pregnant at the time and miscarried while being held in Saint-Lazare Women's Prison.

Leading forensic scientist Dr Léon Thoinot was called in to examine Maurice and the exhumed bodies of the other Weber children but he was unable to confirm that any of them had been strangled. Nevertheless, the rumour spread that Jeanne Weber was a child strangler and she was charged with murder.

Her nine-day trial began on 29 January 1906 at the Cour d'assises de la Seine under Judge Bertulus, which was besieged by angry parents. Jeanne was defended by renowned lawyer Henri-Robert and played the role of a grieving mother. The prosecution had an impressive array of witnesses who testified that the accused had been alone with each of the children when they died. It was also alleged that she had killed her own son Marcel after the deaths of the other Weber children, to divert suspicion.

However, Dr Thoinot swung the jury in Jeanne's favour by saying: 'Science cannot tell you how these children came to die, but everything points to a natural death and that the accused is innocent.' Other expert witnesses testified that there was no conclusive proof that the children had been strangled and the jury then acquitted her, amid the outrage of those in court.

Madame Charles Weber cried 'There is no justice!', while Alphonse Alexandre stood on his seat and yelled: 'She will begin again!'

Jean Weber leapt over the benches to embrace his wife.

'I didn't kill them,' she said. 'Say that you believe me now.'

Differing views

The press were split on the question of her guilt. Noted journalist Michel Durand wrote:

> In the future let no one forget the fate of Jeanne Weber, the fate of an innocent woman, would have been sealed had she not lived in our age and in a Paris which is one of the greatest, if not the greatest, cradles of the exact science of forensic medicine. Science alone has won a victory for innocence and a triumph for itself; for the superiority of scientific knowledge over the testimony of witnesses and the detective work of the police has now been demonstrated.

Le Matin even organized fund-raisers for Jean and Jeanne, who were forced to move out of the Goutte d'Or by hostile neighbours and went to live in a hotel in Boulevard de la Chapelle. On 10 November 1906, a woman who claimed to have been robbed and thrown into the Seine was fished from the river. She gave her name as Jeanne Moulinet, Weber's maiden name. There was another failed suicide attempt on 30 December when she jumped off the bridge at Bercy. But air trapped under her skirt and petticoats kept her afloat until she was pulled from the icy water.

Deadly live-in housekeeper

The story of '*L'Ogresse de la Goutte d'Or*' had been followed by newspapers across France. Farmer Sylvain Bavouzet, a widower in Chambon in the province of Indre, had read it and was convinced of Jeanne Weber's innocence. He then wrote to her, inviting her to come and be his housekeeper. Jean did not fancy starting a new life in the provinces so Jeanne went alone, arriving on 13 March 1907. She took the name Jeanne Glaize and was introduced as the cousin of the late Madame Bavouzet, though she quickly became Bavouzet's mistress.

As well as cooking and cleaning, Jeanne's duties included looking after Bavouzet's children – 16-year-old Germaine, 11-year-old Louise and nine-year-old Auguste, who was said to be full of life. However, on 17 April 1907 he was a little under the weather when he came home from school. The following morning, Bavouzet went to fetch some milk while his two daughters played outside, leaving Jeanne alone with Auguste. When Bavouzet returned, Auguste was dead.

The local physician, Dr Papazoglou, was called. He found the boy's body scrubbed and cleaned and in his best clothes, with the collar buttoned tightly up around his neck.

'Why did you do that?' Dr Papazoglou asked.

'He vomited; he was dirty,' replied the housekeeper.

Dr Papazoglou then noticed the marks around Auguste's neck and refused to sign the death certificate. Instead, he went to the police, who assigned another doctor to the case. After examining the body Dr Charles Audiat then signed the certificate, declaring that Auguste Bavouzet had died of convulsions. The child was buried without any further explanation.

Walks free once again

Germaine Bavouzet was resentful that Jeanne had taken the place of her dead mother in her father's bed, but her papa had sworn the two girls to secrecy. Nevertheless, Germaine confirmed that their new housekeeper was indeed Weber when she found cuttings about the trial in the housekeeper's bag, which contained photographs showing the *Ogresse*. Fearing that she or her younger sister might be her next victims, she took the cuttings to the police.

While the local gendarmes discreetly investigated the case, *Le Matin* got wind of it and sent a journalist to interview Jeanne. Auguste's body was exhumed and bruises and strangulation marks were found around his neck. Meanwhile, the Poyata family and Paul Alexandre, the uncle of little Lucie, filed fresh complaints.

Weber was arrested and incarcerated. Henri-Robert rallied to her defence again and called in Dr Thoinot. He examined the body and questioned the abilities of Dr Bruneau, the provincial physician who had performed the autopsy. Auguste had died of typhoid fever, Thoinot proclaimed. A dispute about the cause of death raged in the academic journals and a third post-mortem was ordered. This proved inconclusive and once again Jeanne Weber walked free.

'Jeanne is free,' wrote one provincial newspaper indignantly, 'and so are Thoinot and Robert.'

Many supporters

Henri-Robert revelled in his victory, telling the Paris Society of Forensic Medicine that Dr Bruneau was an ignorant and inept doctor, while lauding Thoinot.

'After eight months of pre-trial imprisonment, Jeanne Weber was released,' he said. 'You now know who bears responsibility for that imprisonment.'

This damaged Dr Bruneau's career and standing.

Despite the death of one more child in her charge, Weber still had many supporters. She was then seen working as an orderly in a children's hospital in Faucombault, but did not stay there long because of her growing alcoholism. However, George Bonjean, president for the Society for the Protection of Children, gave her a job in a children's home in Orgeville to 'make up for the wrongs that justice has inflicted upon an innocent woman'. She worked there under the name of Marie Lemoine, but a few days after she was hired she was caught with her hands around the neck of a sick child. She was fired, but to maintain the reputation of the institution Bonjean kept quiet about the incident.

Confesses to police

On her return to Paris, Weber was arrested as a vagrant and confessed to the police: 'I am the woman who killed the children in the Goutte d'Or.' However, when she was brought before the Prefect of Police she denied it, so he sent her to the mental asylum in Nanterre, where she was found to be sane and then released. She repeated her confession in Alfortville and narrowly escaped being lynched by a mob. Once more she admitted that she was a murderer to the police who rallied to her protection, but they dismissed her confession as drunken ravings.

She then became the mistress of a man named Joly and lived with him in his lodgings near Toul. Then she turned to prostitution, servicing the railway workers in Bar-le-Duc. She moved to Commercy with one of them, Emile Boucheri, and he and one Jeanne Moulinet took a room in an inn run by a family named Poirot, where Jeanne helped out by looking after the Poirots' six-year-old son Marcel.

On 8 March 1908, Weber told Madame Poirot that her common-law husband was a jealous brute who beat her when he came home drunk and asked if she would let her six-year-old son Marcel sleep with her. That way she would escape a beating.

Caught red-handed

In the night, another guest named Madame Curlet heard loud noises from Weber's room and went to alert the owners. When a knock on the door of Jeanne Moulinet's door garnered no response, Monsieur Poirot opened it with a pass key to discover Weber straddling his son. There was a handkerchief around the boy's neck and blood was flowing from his mouth. Poirot had to hit Weber three times in the face to get her to release her grip on the boy's throat, but Marcel was already dead.

Jeanne was arrested but remained silent. A post-mortem found that she had bitten off the boy's tongue and strangled him with a wet handkerchief. This time there was no doubt that the child had been murdered so there was nothing Henri-Robert or Dr Thoinot could do to save her.

Declared insane

On 25 August 1908 Jeanne Weber was declared insane and locked up in a hospital in Maréville, still protesting her innocence. The public fumed with indignation at the doctors who had allowed the child killer to escape justice and roam free to kill again and meanwhile Jean Weber filed for divorce.

Jeanne Weber was transferred to an asylum at Fains-Véel in Meuse. On 22 April 1909 a rumour spread through La Chapelle that the *Ogresse* had escaped. A woman who looked like her was surrounded by an angry mob and Jean Weber had to be called to confirm that she was not his wife. Then in August there was another panic. *Le Matin* was showing no further interest in Jeanne Weber, but *Le Petit Journal* sent a journalist to the asylum where he found her hospitalized and bedridden.

However, in January 1910 she did escape, but she was only free for a few weeks. She was arrested on 10 February at Châtelier in the Meuse, while she was trying to get a job on a farm in the village.

Weber died on 23 August 1918 during a 'crisis of madness'. A wail of horror came from her cell and when doctors arrived they found she had ripped out her throat with her own nails.

CHAPTER 7

MARIA BOYNE

WHEN 41-YEAR-OLD GRAHAM Boyne was brutally murdered by his 30-year-old wife Maria on the night of 23 April 2008, she was pregnant by her24-year-old lover Gary McGinley. She then took a gold chain from her husband's neck, which she pawned for £220 to pay for a night in a hotel with her boyfriend, who she then tried to frame.

Graham Boyne had not had a pleasant experience of marriage. His first marriage broke down after his wife and his best friend became lovers, so he lost the two people closest to him in one fell swoop. However, his romantic life seemed to revive when he met Maria, who was more than ten years his junior but seemed to take a genuine interest in him.

They married and lived on Parkside Avenue in Barnehurst, a respectable commuter suburb in the London borough of Bexley. Early in the marriage they had two children, but marriage and motherhood were not enough for Maria, who was a shameless flirt and had numerous affairs.

Plans future with lover

Their marital relationship was not helped when Graham lost his job as a TV repairman and consoled himself with drink. Meanwhile, Maria's absences from the marital home grew more frequent. She would disappear for weeks on end, even missing her children's birthdays. Graham soldiered on as a hands-on father and always took Maria back when she returned, but this only invited her contempt and provoked further humiliation.

However, what Maria craved most, along with sex with a series of lovers, was a roof over her head – the one thing that Graham provided. Towards the end of 2007, Maria said she would give the marriage another chance and Graham was delighted. His parents were not over-optimistic that Maria had changed her ways, but at least the couple would be at home for Christmas with their grandchildren. Meanwhile, Graham's father Michael, a retired ambulance man, persuaded him to deal with his increasing dependence on alcohol by seeking help.

Although Maria had returned home, this did not curb her infidelity. She soon took up with 23-year-old warehouseman Gary McGinley. He had learning difficulties and she found him easy to manipulate. While her earlier affairs had been flings, she and Gary began to plan a future together. They would need somewhere to live, however, and Maria told friends that if Graham was no longer around she would have the house. She even told a neighbour that she was considering putting sleeping pills in Graham's vodka to get rid of him once and for all.

Multiple stab wounds

Things came to a head early in 2008 when Maria found herself pregnant with Gary's child. On the evening of 23 April, the lovers checked in to the Holiday Inn in Dartford. That same night, Michael Boyne dropped in at Parkside Avenue to confirm arrangements with

Graham, who was attending an alcohol-addiction clinic the following morning. Later, Gary drove Maria home.

The children were not there that night. Preying on her husband's weakness, Maria sat down with Graham and they had a few drinks together. If they were to revive their marriage, she said, they should spend the night together. She then persuaded him to go upstairs to the bedroom and undress.

He was naked except for his socks when she entered the bedroom with two knives behind her back. She quickly rained down blows on his defenceless body and he suffered 31 stab wounds to his back and sides, as he tried to turn away from his wife's brutal attack.

Maria watched as his life ebbed away, then snatched the gold chain from around his neck and wiped the blood from it. Gary drove her back to Southend, where they pawned the gold chain and then

Boyne rained down blows on her husband's defenceless body.

took a room in a guest house. The proprietor said that they appeared carefree and were laughing and joking. Maria gave the balance of the money to Gary as a present.

Soon after 9 a.m., Michael Boyne turned up at Parkside Avenue. No one answered the door and he could not understand why his son was not ready and waiting. He entered the house and called out, but there was no reply. Puzzled, he went upstairs. In the master bedroom, he found the mutilated body of his son. From his experience as a paramedic he knew that there was nothing he could do to help him.

Police interview Maria

When the police came, the first thing they had to do was contact Maria, as next of kin. No one knew where she was, though a neighbour said they had seen her leaving the house at around 6.15 a.m. That was some three hours before her husband's body had been discovered.

Maria imagined that her stay in Southend had given her some sort of alibi. She tried calling Graham's parents, but got no reply, and then she called her sister, who told her that Graham was dead.

'I know,' she replied.

Gary drove her back to Barnehurst and a little while later she walked into Bexleyheath Police Station, telling the local CID officer that she had nothing to do with the death of her husband. By then an incident room had been set up in Lewisham under Detective Inspector Graeme Gwyn of the Metropolitan Police Force's Homicide and Serious Crime Command.

When interviewed, Maria Boyne maintained that she had been at home with her husband when a man with 'wild staring eyes' broke in. Graham had tackled the intruder and was badly injured, she said. She was asked why she had not called the police? Or an ambulance?

Interviews with friends and family revealed the affair with Gary McGinley and a neighbour said she saw him standing opposite the house at around 11.30 p.m. The police examined phone records and discovered that Maria had no credit left on her mobile phone. However, a call was made from the telephone box nearest the Boynes' house to McGinley's phone at around 1.01 a.m. The caller left a voicemail message which said: 'Have you got a problem? I need to know.'

Lover's statement

When interviewed by the police, Gary said that he had arrived at Parkside Avenue to pick up Maria, not thinking that she had gone ahead with her threat to murder her husband.

'Maria was upset and crying,' he said. 'She said she killed Graham. I didn't believe her at first, then I saw blood on her hands. I went into the house and she was screaming: "What have I done?"'

No neighbour heard her screams.

Gary said he went upstairs and saw Graham covered in blood, lying on the bed. He told the police that Maria said she had killed her husband so they could be together, stressing that she was carrying their child. Consequently, he should do whatever he could to help her. He suggested that they call an ambulance but she vetoed the idea. They then left for Southend.

Both Maria Boyne and Gary McGinley were charged with the murder of Graham Boyne. They appeared at Bexley Magistrates' Court on 28 April 2008 and were held on remand until their trial at the Old Bailey the following February. During that time, Maria gave birth to her third child, which was taken into care.

Gary said that Maria had thrown the knives into the Thames at Erith on their way to Southend and Maria said that Gary had told her to do this. One of the knives was found in the boot of his car and the other was dredged from the river, but it was impossible to determine which was the murder weapon.

Maria accuses lover

Victor Temple QC, prosecuting, said: 'It was a cold-blooded murder. It was a brutal and sustained attack. The marriage was all but over. Divorce was imminent. The only asset was the family home. She was heard from time to time to make threats against her husband with regard to her obtaining the house should he die.'

During the trial Maria retracted her earlier statements and said that Gary McGinley had murdered her husband. She had only lied earlier, she said, because she had been trying to protect her lover and the father of her unborn child. Her story was that it was Gary's idea to get rid of Graham, so they could be together and live in the house.

On the night of the murder, he had called her when she was at home in bed with her husband. After a second call, she had gone downstairs to speak to him on her mobile phone. He said he was waiting outside and she let him in.

When he came in, she could see he had a large carving knife tucked into his waistband.

'You know why I am doing this,' he said, as he hushed her and started going upstairs.

'It did not cross my mind that he would use the knife,' she said. Then she heard Graham cry out: 'Help me!'

Found guilty of murder

On 27 February 2009, after 23 hours' deliberation, the jury found Maria Boyne guilty of murder. Three days later they acquitted Gary McGinley. Maria was given a mandatory life sentence and was told that she must serve a minimum of 24 years before she would be considered for parole.

Judge Paul Worsley, who described Boyne as 'scheming and devious', said that her husband had been a vulnerable man.

He was the father of your two young children and long-suffering and forgiving of your repeated infidelities with different men. And he took you back when you chose to return to him and your children. But in April 2008, pregnant with your lover's child, you decided to get your hands on the family home. This was a murder with a view to gain. You repeatedly told others that you had intended to get your hands on the house and to do whatever it took to achieve that aim. You were also motivated by sex and selfishness . . . I'm satisfied that you enticed your husband to go to bed naked on the pretext of sex. You rained 31 blows upon his chest and back with that knife. At some stage he tried to defend himself. You showed him no mercy.

Family's lives torn apart

Graham Boyne was not the only victim of the crime. On 23 February, Michael Boyne told his wife Joan and daughter Elaine to attend court without him as he felt too unwell to travel. They returned home to find that he had collapsed. He died in hospital the following day.

Judge Paul Worsley said: 'You left Graham's father to discover the bloodied corpse of his son. That was unforgivable. It is thanks only to the love and care of Graham Boyne's mother and father that your two children have not been put with strangers to care for them. You have effectively rendered them orphans.'

Although Michael Boyne was dead, his written statement was read to the court. In it, he said his granddaughter, aged eight, had 'run round the house and was inconsolable. She said she wanted to die so she could be with her daddy.' His grandson, aged six, wanted to know if his daddy would ever come back.

Assessing the situation, Michael Boyne said: 'The marriage was on the rocks, but my son thought the world of her, despite her many affairs.'

He said that his son did not want to finish their marriage.

'Our lives have been torn apart and the children cannot comprehend how anyone would have wanted to harm their daddy,' Michael Boyne said. 'Since that day, we have had to come to terms with the fact that we will never see him or hear his voice again. We were very proud of our son. He was hard-working, conscientious and very sociable. As a family we will always be haunted by imagining the last moments of Graham's life. Did he suffer?'

Detective Inspector Gwyn gave his own assessment.

This was a savage attack motivated ultimately by the desire of Maria Boyne to live in her former marital home. The cold-hearted murder of Graham has devastated his family and Maria Boyne's actions have left two young children without a father and their mother facing a substantial prison sentence. Throughout this investigation and trial Maria Boyne constructed a self-serving and complex web of deceit, which the jury were able to see through in reaching their verdict.

CHAPTER 8

ANNA MARIE HAHN

THE PRESS DUBBED Anna Marie Hahn 'The Blonde Borgia' after the Renaissance femme fatale Lucrezia Borgia, famed for poisoning dinner guests with lethal doses administered from a hollow ring – though there is no historic evidence that she did any such thing. Anna Marie Hahn certainly did though. At the age of 32, she was the first woman to die in the electric chair in Ohio. She had been sentenced to death for the murder of 78-year-old Jacob Wagner, though the prosecution linked her to the deaths of at least five elderly men, whom she also robbed, using a variety of poisons. In court, much attention was paid to her elegant attire and beautiful coiffure. However, she lost some of it when a patch was shaved to attach the electrode from Old Sparky in Ohio State Penitentiary.

Arrested on suspicion

Her crimes were discovered when another elderly man, 67-year-old George Obendorfer, died at the Memorial Hospital in Colorado Springs on 1 August 1937. The doctors could not ascertain a cause of death so the police were called in to investigate.

When he was taken ill, Obendorfer had been staying at the Park Hotel, whose owner had just filed a report concerning the theft of $300 worth of diamonds (some $5,000 now). According to the register, Obendorfer was from Cincinnati, Ohio, and had registered with Anna Hahn and her young son Oskar, also from Cincinnati. However, when their rooms were checked, there was no sign of her. Detectives discovered that a woman answering Hahn's description had been trying to pawn jewellery and withdraw $1,000 ($15,000 now) from a Denver bank using Obendorfer's bank book. She claimed to be Mrs Obendorfer, but detectives were convinced that she was Anna Hahn.

Once back in Cincinnati, she was arrested. At first, she claimed not to know Obendorfer but when she was reminded that she had checked in to the Park Hotel in Colorado Springs with him, she claimed that she had only met him on the train and was trying to help him. However, according to Obendorfer's family the couple had planned to travel to Colorado together to view a ranch she said she owned. During their interviews, the police looked further into her background.

Marriage

Born Anna Marie Filser in Bavaria in 1906, she had emigrated to the United States in 1929 with her husband, a Viennese doctor, and their son Oskar. Her husband died soon after they arrived in Cincinnati, but Anna decided to stay on. At a dance in the city's German district, she met Philip Hahn. They married and went into business running delicatessens. After a fire in one of their shops, Anna collected $300 from the insurance company. Two fires in their marital home netted a further $2,000 and the police began to suspect she was an arsonist.

Then she attempted to persuade her husband to take out life insurance for $25,000, but he refused. Nevertheless, Philip Hahn soon fell desperately ill and his mother took him to hospital against Anna's wishes. He survived the mysterious illness, but the couple separated shortly afterwards. Anna then supported herself by nursing elderly patients, though she had no previous experience in the field.

Deadly nurse

Detectives found that Anna Hahn had been nursing retired gardener Jacob Wagner, who had died mysteriously two months before Obendorfer, leaving his entire estate to Anna Hahn. They learned that she had claimed to be his long-lost niece, though he had no living relatives. Neighbours said that she spent hours in his apartment after his death. Not only that, but a lady in his block whom Hahn had befriended fell violently ill after eating an ice cream that Hahn had given her. While she was in hospital, money and jewellery was stolen from her apartment. And when Wagner's body was exhumed it was found to contain high levels of arsenic.

After seeing reports in the press, 62-year-old George Heis then came forward, saying that a year before he had fallen violently ill after Hahn, his carer, had poured a beer for him. He became suspicious when two houseflies that had sampled the brew dropped dead. When she refused a taste, he sacked her. Though he continued to suffer after-effects, he survived to testify against her.

Weeks before she travelled to Colorado, another of her patients, 77-year-old George Gsellman, had fallen ill and died. When his body was exhumed it was found to contain a large amount of croton oil – a diarrhoea medicine that can kill in large doses. Philip Hahn then handed over a bottle of croton oil that he had taken from his wife. A local pharmacist, who knew Anna personally, confirmed that she had bought it.

During a search of her home, the police found an IOU for $2,000. She had apparently borrowed money from 72-year-old Albert Palmer, who died while she was nursing him through a lengthy illness. After

Hahn claimed she had met Obendorfer by chance on a train, but the truth was she had bought him his ticket at Union Terminal, Cincinnati.

his death she had kept the money and taken back the note. According to relatives, a further $4,000 was missing from his estate.

When Anna's son Oskar was questioned, he contradicted his mother's story that they had met Obendorfer by chance on the train. Instead, she had bought his ticket in Union Terminal, Cincinnati. She had also given him several drinks on the train and he had begun to feel ill before they arrived in Colorado.

Charged with murder

There was a warrant for 'grand larceny' out for her in Colorado, in connection with the diamonds. However, instead of shipping her back there, the authorities in Ohio decided to charge her with the murder of Jacob Wagner, using the other mysterious deaths as corroborating evidence.

In court, witnesses were called to give evidence about Wagner's agonizing end. A chemist testified that he had found enough arsenic in his body to kill four men and a handwriting expert said that Wagner's will was a forgery. The handwriting was Hahn's.

Hahn took the stand in her own defence. She denied the accusations, and could not be tripped up in cross-examination, but there was little she could do to contest the forensic evidence against her. The prosecutor, Dudley Outcalt, sealed her fate with his closing statement, saying:

> She is sly, because she developed her relationships with old men who had no relatives and lived alone. She is avaricious, because no act was so low but that she was ready to commit it for slight gain. She is cold-blooded, like no other woman in the world, because no one could sit here for four weeks and hear this damaging parade of evidence and display no emotion. She is heartless, because nobody with a heart could deal out the

death she dealt these old men. We've seen here the coldest, most heartless cruel person that ever has come within the scope of our lives. In the four corners of this courtroom stand four dead men. Gsellman, Palmer, Wagner, Obendorfer! From the four corners bony fingers point at her and say: 'That woman poisoned me! That woman made my last moments an agony! That woman tortured me with the tortures of the damned!' Then, turning to you they say: 'Let my death be not entirely in vain. My life cannot be brought back, but through my death and the punishment to be inflicted upon her, you can prevent such a death from coming to another man.' From the four corners of this room, those old men say to you, 'Do your duty!' I ask of you, for the state of Ohio, that you withhold any recommendations of mercy.

The attorney for the defence, Joseph H. Hoodin, had little to counter this.

I will not say that a single witness lied, but this case has had such widespread publicity that it would have been impossible for these witnesses not to have preconceived ideas before they ever came into this courtroom. Particularly this is true of the witnesses from Wagner's neighbourhood, where the case has been the chief topic of conversation for months. Although she is no angel, she is not guilty of the murder of Jacob Wagner.

Sentenced to death

The jury of 11 women and one man were not convinced by this. They took just two hours to return a verdict of guilty, with no recommendation for mercy. This meant an automatic sentence of death. Before formally sentencing her on 10 November 1937, Judge Charles S. Bell asked Hahn if she had anything to say.

'I have,' she replied. 'I am innocent, your honour.'

Judge Bell then said:

It is ordered, adjudged, and desired by the court that the defendant, Anna Marie Hahn, be taken hence to jail in Hamilton County, Ohio, and that within 30 days hereof the Sheriff of Hamilton County shall convey the said defendant to the Ohio penitentiary and deliver her to the warden thereof, and that on the tenth day of March, 1938 the said warden shall cause a current of electricity sufficient to cause death to pass through the body of the said defendant, the application of such current to be continued until the said defendant is dead.

Then he turned to Hahn and said: 'And may God, in his infinite wisdom, have mercy on your soul.'

Appeals went all the way up to the US Supreme Court, to no avail. On 6 December 1938, it was announced that the execution would take place at 8 p.m. the following day. In the time left to her, Hahn wrote four letters which she handed to her attorney. One contained her confession, which was sold to the *Cincinnati Enquirer*. The money was put in trust for Oskar's education.

Confession

I don't know how I could have done the things I did in my life. Only God knows what came over me when I gave Albert Palmer, that first one, that poison that caused his death. Up in heaven there is a God who will judge. He will know and

He will tell me how it came about. He will tell me what caused me to do the same things to Mr. Wagner and the last one, Mr. Obendorfer. I never knew myself afterwards, and I don't know now.

When those poor men were sick I tried to do everything for them. When I stood by Mr. Wagner as he was laid out at the funeral home I don't know how it was I didn't scream out at the top of my voice. I couldn't in my mind believe that it was me, Anna Marie Hahn, who loved people so well and wanted friends all the time, that could have put Mr. Wagner there. I can't believe it even today. I couldn't believe it when in the court those people came to the room and told the jury how they said these men died. I was sitting there hearing a story like out of a book all about another person.

As things come to my mind now and as I put them on this paper I can't believe I am writing about things I did myself. However, they must be about me because they are in my mind and I know them. God above will tell me what made me do these terrible things. I couldn't have been in my right mind when I did them. I loved all people so much. Now I am so close to death. Death is all around me. I have been here [on Death Row] for what seems another lifetime already. Several other people in this place have been called out.

She went on to give an account of her younger days in Germany and then described how her early setbacks in the US had led her into a life of crime.

My husband and I had been out of work and I started worrying about my boy's future. I became crazy with fears that my boy and I would starve. I signed some notes for my husband,

Brand-new state-of-the-art Death Row at Ohio Penitentiary in 1938. Hahn met her end in the room where the electric chair was kept, behind the door you can see at the end of the corridor.

because I had signed these notes they threatened to take my Colerain Avenue house away from me, to sell the house over my head and throw me and my boy out into the street. Then it was that I started gambling and playing the racehorses. I wanted to make some money for my boy.

Hahn met Palmer at the racetrack. She borrowed money from him.

I paid much of it back. Then when I didn't pay it back fast enough to suit him, then it was that he wanted me to be his girl. He threatened me that if I didn't do what he asked he would get his attorney to get the rest of the money that I borrowed from him. He wouldn't leave me alone. God knows that I did not want to kill him, and I don't know what put such a thought in my head. I remembered that down in the cellar was some rat poison. Something in my mind kept saying to me, 'Give him a little of this and he won't trouble you anymore'.

She put the poison in his oysters and told him to go home. Later she visited him in hospital and prayed he would get well. When he died, 'only I knew why'.

Still short of money, she had stolen some of Jacob Wagner's bank books. When he found out, she was frightened he would report her.

I got scared that if the police would start questioning me maybe all this about Mr. Palmer would come out. Something cried out in me to stop him, so that all my troubles wouldn't start again. I don't know what guided my hand, but I fixed him some orange juice and placed a half of teaspoon of the powder poison, which I took from my purse, in the glass.

She claimed that she did not kill Wagner for his money. Forging his will was an afterthought, she said. She also admitted killing George Gsellman and George Obendorfer, but did not give details.

> I have written this confession with the full knowledge that death is near, and I only ask one favour and that is that my son should not be judged for the wrongs his mother may have done.

The confession was signed Anna Marie Hahn.

Anna Marie Hahn claimed she did not kill Wagner for his money and that forging his will was an afterthought.

Execution

Once all of the appeals were exhausted, Anna Marie Hahn was escorted
from her cell with one of her counsels and her three matrons. As she
was marched through the death house, the 12 convicted men awaiting
their own executions paid their respects.

'Goodbye all of you and God bless you,' she said.

Approaching the door of the execution chamber, she stumbled
and two guards had to pick her up and put her in the chair. Only then
did she beg for mercy. Turning to the prison warden, she said: 'Mr
Woodward, don't do this to me. Think of my boy. Can't you think of
my baby?'

Then she addressed the witnesses to her execution, saying: 'Isn't
there anybody who will help me? Is nobody going to help me?'

'I'm sorry, but we have to do it, Mrs Hahn,' replied the warden.

She beckoned to the chaplain, the Reverend John Sullivan, saying:
'Father, come close.'

He gripped her hand, but she whispered between sobs: 'Be careful,
father. You will be killed.'

The Reverend Sullivan then intoned the Lord's Prayer as the
current crackled through her body at 8.10 p.m. on 7 December 1938.
Three minutes later she was declared dead.

CHAPTER 9

EDITH MCALINDEN

THE TOP-FLOOR FLAT on Dixon Avenue in the Crosshill district of Glasgow, Scotland became known as the 'House of Blood'. Inside, the police found three bodies of men who had been brutally slain. One of them was cradled in the arms of a woman who was crying, 'Wake up, wake up! Don't do this to me!' and blood and human tissue dripped from the walls and the ceiling. Detective Superintendent Willie Johnstone, a veteran of 30 years' service, said: 'The crime scene was the most chilling I have ever visited.'

He was on duty in the early hours of 17 October 2004 when he received a call informing him that 37-year-old Edith McAlinden was in custody.

She said that a fight had broken out between her boyfriend, 42-year-old David Gillespie, and the two residents of the flat, Anthony Coyle, 71, and Ian Mitchell, 67, whom she called 'Pops'. The violence had been fuelled by alcohol after a prolonged drinking session.

The flat belonged to Mitchell, a retired joiner. For ten years, he had rented out his spare room to Coyle, a retired labourer originally from Donegal but a resident of Glasgow for most of his adult life.

Both were heavy drinkers and known troublemakers, though they were well liked. Gillespie was a more recent acquaintance.

Pleads innocence

McAlinden claimed to have found the three men already dead but the flat was in such a state that it was impossible to make out how any fight had started. The place was full of empty bottles, the furniture was smashed and there was a bewildering array of weapons – knives, an axe, a hammer, a golf club, a baseball bat, wooden slats, an electric drill. Even an electric kettle had played some part in the mayhem.

When the paramedics arrived, McAlinden would not let go of Gillespie's body so they could attend to him. Nor would she stop screaming. When a police officer intervened, she lashed out at him and had to be handcuffed and arrested for breach of the peace. Her records showed she was an inveterate offender with convictions for theft, prostitution, affray and assault. She had recently been released from prison, having served nine months for a serious assault, only to resume her life as a homeless drifter.

At around 3 a.m. on the morning of the incident, she went to neighbour James Sweeney's house and told him that something had happened at Mitchell's flat. She then begged Sweeney to go back with her and check the situation out. When he went to the flat and saw the state of the hallway he ventured no further and immediately called the emergency services on his mobile.

Gillespie had recently separated from the mother of his three daughters, 45-year-old Violet Cahill. McAlinden said she had taken him up to Mitchell's flat, a place he had visited two or three times before. The three of them had a few drinks together and McAlinden said she then went out to get more supplies. When she got back, Coyle had returned and a fight must have broken out, but she did not know what had caused it. Then she ran to fetch Sweeney.

McAlinden was an inveterate offender with convictions for theft, prostitution, affray and assault.

Appalling sight

As the forensic team moved into the flat, the procurator fiscal responsible for investigating sudden or suspicious deaths asked to visit the crime scene. However, the sight she beheld was so appalling that she could not stay.

Listing the men's injuries took hours. The two older men had suffered repeated blunt-force trauma and had also been scalded with boiling water from the kettle that sat in the middle of the room.

Gillespie had received two grievous knife wounds to the leg. These had severed his femoral artery. His blood had been thinned by cider and strong wine and, too drunk to help himself, he had lain on the sofa and bled to death.

None of this seemed to add up. The sofa was soaked with blood, indicating that Gillespie had not moved after he had been stabbed. In that case, who had attacked the other two men? And who had poured boiling water over them? Under interrogation, McAlinden stuck to her story – that a fight had broken out and the men had been killed while she was out of the room. Clearly, she was a suspect, but it seemed unlikely that she could have carried out the three murders by herself. The police then searched for a likely accomplice and quickly found one – her 16-year-old son John.

Fearsome reputation

Edith McAlinden had been on the streets from the age of ten and she was 20 when John was born. Little was known of his father and he seems to have played no part in John's upbringing. She struggled to provide for him and appears to have supplemented her income as a prostitute by robbing her drunken clients. Few dared complain; she had a fearsome reputation.

John stuck by his mother. When she came out of prison shortly before the murders, he took her out on a drinking session with his best friend, 16-year-old Jamie Gray, who was so close that John called him 'brother'. Like his mother, John was homeless and living in a hostel at the time. He and Jamie had also been in trouble with the law for petty theft and fighting but, again like his mother, he could handle himself.

For Edith, Pops was a ready source of money, drink and, sometimes, shelter. On his side, she was an opportunity to have sex with a younger woman who was not bad looking. Coyle thought that Mitchell was being exploited, so when she came around he usually made himself scarce.

Witnesses killed

What happened on the night of the murders was pieced together later. Coyle, it seems, was down at the pub when McAlinden and Gillespie arrived at Mitchell's flat. He had little alternative but to let them in, knowing they would only stay until the drink ran out.

But something went wrong. Perhaps some flippant remark was taken the wrong way. Leaving Gillespie on the sofa, McAlinden got up and went into the kitchen. She returned with a knife and stabbed him in the legs. The rapid blood loss from the femoral artery would have plunged him into shock. He was incapacitated and was so drunk that he did not realize he was dying. His two companions were equally intoxicated.

It eventually dawned on McAlinden that she risked going back to jail, so something had to be done. She asked Mitchell for some money, then went to the telephone – but not to call an ambulance. Instead, she called her son John.

Nearly 40 minutes later, John and Jamie turned up in a taxi and Edith paid it off with Mitchell's money. It seems that in her phone call Edith told John that Mitchell had tried to rape her. The two teenagers were fired up and they had brought weapons with them.

Mitchell tried to defend himself – the injuries to his arms testified to that – but the two boys bludgeoned him with a baseball bat and a slat of wood. They kicked him and beat him beyond recognition and eventually he began choking on his own blood.

At this point Coyle returned home. Quickly seeing that something was wrong, he fled into his bedroom, but he could not call for help as he had no mobile phone. The bedroom door withstood the boys' attempt to kick it in, so they got Mitchell's electric drill and tried to remove the hinges. That failed too.

Edith then took a hand. Through the door, she could hear Coyle praying. She told him that there had been a terrible mistake. The boys had gone and she needed his help. He could not leave her alone with Mitchell and she did not know what to do. He might die.

Coyle fell for it and opened the bedroom door. As he emerged, the two boys fell on him. He tried to crawl along the passageway, but as he went they smashed his skull in with a golf club. He too tried to defend himself, but the situation was hopeless.

The two witnesses to the murders now appeared to be dead. But how could they be sure? First they put a cushion over what was left of Coyle's face and stood on it. Edith then told John to put the kettle on. They watched as she poured boiling water over the lifeless bodies of Mitchell and Coyle. They did not move, so the killers could be sure they were dead.

Charged with murder

McAlinden then told John and Jamie to leave and she would sort things out. Preparing her story about there having been a fight, she went to see Sweeney. When interviewed by the police, she stuck to this tale. However, witnesses had seen two young men making their way from a cab into the building in Dixon Avenue.

The police also heard from Bryan Gallagher, another resident of the hostel where John McAlinden was staying. He said that McAlinden had boasted to him about a murder, saying: 'Stabbed a guy in the legs, man. There was blood everywhere. It was a fella tried to rape my ma. So I had to teach him a lesson, eh.'

John and Jamie were brought in for questioning. They said they had been in Dixon Avenue earlier in the evening, but had no idea what had happened after they left.

Their story seemed plausible enough and it seemed unlikely that two 16-year-olds who had previously only been involved in petty crime would have committed such a horrific attack. However, the forensic evidence contradicted their story. Although their clothes had been cleaned, there were still traces of blood on them. They gave minimal statements and showed no remorse. All three – Edith, John and Jamie – were charged with all three murders.

Life sentences

The trial started seven months later in May 2005, with the defendants pleading not guilty. The prosecution called Isher Singh Dass, a bus driver who lived in the flat below Mitchell's. He said that a few hours before the bodies of Gillespie, Mitchell and Coyle were found he heard a 'noise like thunder' and the ceiling shook.

Mitchell's 38-year-old son was asked whether he had ever met Edith McAlinden, the accused. He replied: 'Three or four times. She was in the flat when I went to see my dad.' But he was not clear what the relationship between them was.

The prosecution then showed the court the police video of the carnage in the flat. The defendants laughed, but the jury were ashen-faced. Defence counsel then persuaded the defendants to change their plea.

Cleverly, they each admitted one murder only. Edith McAlinden pleaded guilty to the murder of David Gillespie, John McAlinden admitted to killing Ian Mitchell and Jamie Gray said he was responsible for Tony Coyle's death. This ensured that they each received a lighter sentence than admitting all three as charged.

All three received a mandatory life sentence, with Edith McAlinden being given a minimum tariff of 13 years while the two boys were handed a minimum tariff of 12 years. Passing sentence, the judge, Lady Justice Dorrian, said of Edith McAlinden:

> I recognize that you were initially charged with three murders whereas the Crown have accepted a plea to one murder and that in very different terms from the way in which it was originally charged. In all the circumstances I fix the punishment part at 13 years. In doing so, I have taken account of the fact that you tendered a plea of guilty, which although tendered during trial, nevertheless cut short what would otherwise have been a much longer trial. And I have reduced the punishment part from the 14 years which I would otherwise have imposed.

Gillespie's former partner, Violet Cahill, who had remained on good terms with him after they split, said: 'I am just disgusted, yet they go down the stairs laughing as if the whole thing is a big joke. There are animals on the street better than these people. They are scum. My children stay up crying all night because they've lost their dad.'

On her arrival at the women's prison, HMP Cornton Vale, McAlinden boasted about being the woman from the House of Blood – but not for long. Other prisoners took her aside and administered their own punishment. Later, though, McAlinden embarked on a series of lesbian affairs with many women including Michelle Morrow, a drug dealer, and the murderer Pamela Gourlay.

She also stayed in touch with her son by letter, telling him to 'Keep the grin above the chin'. They were, she said, both part of the 'Anti-screw crew 110%'.

CHAPTER 10
MARIE ALEXANDRINE BECKER

LIÈGE HOUSEWIFE MARIE Alexandrine Becker lived a blameless life until she was 55. Then she began a spree of murder, theft and forgery. The profits she made from her crimes were squandered on a series of young lovers.

Her crimes came to light when an old woman died of 'acute indigestion'. There was nothing immediately suspicious about her death and a doctor and a nurse were present. However, a complaint had been made on a report that passed across the desk of the Police Commissioner, Honore Lebrun, on 3 October 1935. He was immediately struck by the name of the deceased's nurse, Marie Becker. Her name had appeared on two other recent reports of women who had died from 'acute indigestion'. Was this just a coincidence? He set up an investigation.

Mrs Becker had been born Marie Alexandrine Petitjean to a family of poor farm workers in Wamont, in the Flemish-speaking region of Belgium, in 1877. An ambitious woman, she wanted more out of life than toiling on a farm. A local priest taught her reading, writing and arithmetic and at 16 she left home to take up an apprenticeship in dressmaking in Liège.

Lavished gifts on lovers

While still young, she married Charles Becker, who owned a sawmill. Later he invested in a furniture factory. Marie used her dressmaking skills to copy the latest fashions from Paris but she craved more. She had a series of young lovers and took up with middle-aged rake Lambert Beyer, who made her acquaintance when she was buying vegetables at a market stall. Her staid and reliable husband stood in the way of this tempestuous romance but in 1932 he died of 'acute indigestion'. She collected on his life insurance and invested the money in a dress shop. But she soon tired of Beyer and he died too, leaving her more money.

Becker was then seen dancing wildly with men at the local nightclubs, outraging the respectable ladies of Liège. Often she would pay young gigolos to escort her home and take her to bed. Her particular favourite was the handsome Maximilian Houdy, 20 years her junior, on whom she lavished expensive gifts. But the business failed and soon she was short of money.

First brush with the law

One day in March 1933, she went to the cinema with Marie Doupagne-Castaldot, who agreed to loan her 19,000 Belgian francs. Afterwards, they went for a drink together. Doupagne-Castaldot then fell ill and Becker offered to look after her, but under Becker's care her symptoms soon grew worse and she died. An anonymous letter was sent to the prosecutor's office, which prompted a report that ended up on the Commissioner's desk, and Becker was arrested. She had apparently nursed a number of other elderly friends who suffered a similar fate.

'It seems that those who entrust themselves to your care have an undeviating tendency to die suddenly,' the investigating magistrate declared.

'But they are old,' Becker replied. 'What would you have? Is it not that everyone dies so, sooner or later?'

'That is true,' said the magistrate. 'But also it is possible for the old to die before their time. I understand that you invariably served your patients tea, and justice demands that you inform me what you put into the tea.'

'Herbs,' said Becker. 'Only herbs of the most beneficent kinds. Herbs that would have healed them if it was that they were to live.'

String of murders

However, there was no direct evidence to support a charge of murder and Becker was released. Instead of regarding this brush with the law as a warning, Becker continued working for rich, elderly women whose mortality rate was suspiciously high. It was later discovered that if she did not acquire money by directly stealing from her victims she got it by forging their wills or otherwise obtaining money by fraud.

When she ran out of elderly friends, she turned to the customers of the boutique she had invested in. Victims would be invited into a back room of the shop to discuss the latest fashions and she would offer them a cup of tea or a glass of wine. She would then accompany them home, where she took over as nurse, with the same results as before.

One such was Marie-Louise Evrard-Crulle, who died on 11 November 1935. Relatives noted to their astonishment that she had left her money to a young man who was completely unknown to them. It turned out that the heir was a close friend of Marie Becker. A second anonymous letter then turned up at the prosecutor's office, accusing Becker of murder and the misappropriation of the inheritance.

Marie Becker – it seemed that those who entrusted themselves to her care had an 'undeviating tendency' to die suddenly.

Although doctors ascribed the death to hepatic colic, which had triggered a heart attack, Becker remained under surveillance.

More evidence accrued and then Madame Guichner contacted the police. She said she had complained to Becker about her husband, saying: 'I wish he were dead.'

Becker then replied: 'If you really mean that, I can supply you with a powder that will leave no trace.' She disposed of ten to 12 old ladies this way and even attended their funerals, where she was seen dressed in black and kneeling at the graveside in tears. After leaving the cemetery, she would scurry off to spend their money on young men.

Caught in the act

On 30 September 1936, she went to the funeral of Madame Lange with Madame Weiss and Madame Lamy, inviting them to her home afterwards. Madame Weiss died a few hours later. The police then asked Madame Lamy to invite Becker round to her house. When Becker arrived, she was arrested and the police found a bottle of digitalis in her handbag.

'I suffered from heart trouble,' she explained, 'and I had to take it. I did not want my lover to know.'

In small doses, digitalis is used to cure cardiac arrhythmia, but an overdose can kill, producing symptoms like those of acute indigestion. When doctors examined Madame Becker they could find nothing wrong with her heart. As the judge later put it: 'In spite of your heart trouble you were known to go to dance halls and behave like a strong and flirtatious young woman. The druggist and chemist you name are dead, but the police have found no entries of your case in their registers.'

When the police visited Becker and searched her home, they found clothing, jewellery and other items belonging to her victims, along with a bag Madame Weiss had used to keep 40,000 Belgian francs in. Meanwhile, a panel of experts had to study the effects of digitalis to prove it was a credible murder weapon.

Found guilty of murder

Becker spent 17 months in prison, while the bodies of her victims were exhumed. Traces of digitalis were found in all of them. The indictment was 12,000 words long and took the court clerk three hours to read out. In the packed courtroom Becker was faced with ten lawyers, 1,800 items of evidence and 294 witnesses, every one of whose statements she contested.

'Everyone in the case is lying except you?' asked the judge.

'Yes,' she replied, nodding vigorously.

Throughout she maintained the pose of an innocent woman who had been wronged by these accusations. She kept asking the judge to hurry as she had other matters to attend to but his response was that she had yet to clear herself.

One explanation of Becker's middle-aged murder spree is that she was trying to recapture her lost youth. It was reported that she appeared in court made up gaudily and dressed like a 16-year-old flapper. A dozen former teenage lovers testified that she had lavished money and presents on them and she was forced to admit that this left her always in need of money. In her defence, she said: 'As for my going out with young people, my theory has always been that one is as young as one thinks oneself to be. As for what little money I spent on my friends from time to time, well, somehow Providence always saw to it that I was well cared for in worldly things. I seldom worried.'

Distraught as Becker had seemed at the funerals of her victims, in the dock she gloated over her crimes. She said one victim, Madame Lambert, 'looked like an angel choked with sauerkraut', while she saw Madame Doupagne-Castaldot 'dying beautifully, lying flat on her back'.

Marie Alexandrine Becker was found guilty of 11 murders and sentenced to death. However, in Belgium the death sentence is automatically commuted to life imprisonment. She died in jail in 1942, aged 61.

CHAPTER 11

KRISTEN GILBERT

KRISTEN GILBERT WAS known as a skilled nurse who remained calm in medical emergencies. She won the admiration of those that worked alongside her at the Veterans Administration Medical Center in Northampton, Massachusetts. But in 1990, after she returned from maternity leave, it was noted that the rate of cardiac arrests on Ward C was three times greater than it had been over the previous three years. Patients were dying of cardiac arrest even though they had not suffered from heart complaints previously. So many of them were under the care of Kristen Gilbert that her co-workers began to call her the 'Angel of Death'. At first, it was a joke.

Born Kristen Heather Strickland in Fall River, Massachusetts, in 1967, she showed signs as a teenager of being a pathological liar. For one, she made unfounded claims about being a distant relation of the infamous Lizzie Borden, who reputedly despatched her mother and father with 40 whacks in Fall River in 1892, though she was acquitted.

Former boyfriends accused her of being strange and controlling. They said she even resorted to verbal and physical abuse, or tampering with their cars. When all else failed, she would fake suicide attempts.

Graduating from high school a year and a half early, she enrolled in Bridgewater State College and majored in pre-med, though she later transferred to Greenfield Community College to be closer to her future husband, Glenn Gilbert. While working as a home health aide, she once badly scalded a child with learning difficulties, though no action was taken against her. No one suspected that it might have been deliberate. Then in 1988 she became a registered nurse and eloped with Glenn Gilbert. Their marriage was full of rows, however, and on one occasion she chased him around the house with a butcher's knife.

Soon after their marriage, Kristen got a job at the Veterans Administration Medical Center in Northampton, Massachusetts, working on Ward C. Well liked, she remembered birthdays and organized gift exchanges during the holidays. She distinguished herself early on and was featured in the magazine *VA Practitioner* in April 1990.

Deaths start to climb

Everything changed after the birth of her first child, when she was switched to the 4 p.m. to midnight shift. Deaths during her shifts then began to climb, though she still showed skill and confidence during these emergencies. However, one doctor refused to let her treat any more of his patients.

After the birth of her second son in 1993, the Gilberts' marriage ran into difficulties. She had taken a fancy to James Perrault, a security guard at the hospital.

Under VA rules, security had to be on hand during any medical emergency, so when there was a cardiac arrest on Ward C he would be called, giving her the chance to impress him with her medical skills and flirt with him. They would also have drinks together after her shift ended.

Gilbert seemed to be an exemplary employee but when she changed shifts, the death rate went up.

When they became lovers, it was alleged that an AIDS patient suddenly died of a heart attack so that she could leave early to go on a date with Perrault. Gilbert's husband Glenn then found his food tasted odd and was convinced that she was trying to kill him. Soon afterwards, Kristen moved out of the marital home to be closer to Perrault and she then filed for divorce.

The high mortality rate on Ward C put all the nurses under suspicion. While the authorities were searching for some explanation, it was noted that stocks of the drug epinephrine – a synthetic form of adrenaline – were going missing. It was a heart stimulant that could cause cardiac arrest if injected unnecessarily. Three fellow nurses then reported their suspicions to the authorities.

Hoax bomb calls

While the matter was under investigation, Gilbert bought a device to disguise her voice and then called the hospital to say that bombs had been planted there. Staff and patients, many of whom were sick and elderly, had to be evacuated. No explosives were found, but the hoax calls always occurred on Perrault's shift.

It was not long before the police linked Gilbert to the calls. Perrault was then summoned before a grand jury, where he testified against his lover. At that point, Glenn Gilbert asked investigators to come to his house and search Kristen's former pantry, where they found the *Handbook of Poisoning*. Meanwhile, Gilbert was temporarily placed in a psychiatric ward at Arbour Hospital for the third time in a month.

She later turned up at Glenn Gilbert's house and threatened him with her car keys. A court order then confined her to Bayside Medical Center. When she was released, she was arrested on a charge of making bomb threats. She was then sentenced to 15 months at Danbury Federal Prison and treated for psychiatric problems.

Patients' bodies exhumed

While she was in prison, investigators began to exhume some of the bodies of those who had died on her shift. They were found to contain epinephrine, though the deceased patients had no history of heart complaints.

In November 1998, aged 30, she was indicted for the murders of four men and the attempted murders of three others. However, the United States attorney said that 37 men had died during her shifts between January 1995 and February 1996. Her potential body count was much greater. In the seven years she had worked at the VA hospital, 350 patients had died on her shifts and she was thought to have been responsible for 80 of the deaths.

In all the prosecution brought 70 witnesses and 200 pieces of evidence against her.

The witnesses included her ex-husband, who said she had confessed to the murders.

Perrault also testified against her, saying that she had told him during a telephone conversation: 'I did it. You wanted to know, I killed all those guys by injection.'

The defence maintained that she had only said that after suffering psychiatric problems following the break-up of their tempestuous affair. There were no witnesses to Gilbert administering the drug, so all the evidence was circumstantial.

'The four murders were especially cruel and heinous,' said US Attorney David Stern, citing the case of 41-year-old Kenneth Cutting, who was blind and had multiple sclerosis. Gilbert had asked a supervisor if she could leave work early if he were to die. He died 40 minutes later and empty ampoules of epinephrine were found nearby. Prosecutors maintained that Gilbert was also on duty when 37 of the 63 patients on Ward C died and that she tried to cover her tracks by falsifying medical records.

Explaining why Gilbert was standing trial in just seven cases, Assistant US Attorney Ariane Vuono told jurors: 'These seven victims were veterans. They were vulnerable. They were the perfect victims. When Kristen Gilbert killed them, she used the perfect poison.'

Lawyers for Gilbert argued that the patients died of natural causes. They said Gilbert had been falsely accused by her co-workers, who were upset that she was having an extramarital affair.

'She was scorned by her peers and her co-workers,' defence attorney David Hoose told the jury. 'You must understand how rumours about what was going on in Kristen Gilbert's life affected, coloured and tainted everyone's opinions of what was going on in Ward C.'

Life imprisonment

Despite her lawyers' pleas, in March 2001 Kristen Gilbert was found guilty of three counts of first-degree murder, one count of second-degree murder and two counts of attempted murder. While there was no death penalty in the state of Massachusetts, the crimes had taken place on federal property, so she faced the prospect of execution – ironically, by lethal injection. Assistant US Attorney William Welch called Gilbert a 'shell of a human being' who deserved to die for the cold and calculating way she murdered her victims.

The defence argued that she did not need to die, because it would be punishment enough to lead a life 'where you can't walk out into a field, or see snow or play with a puppy'. Her father and grandmothers also pleaded for her life, saying a death sentence would be devastating to them and Gilbert's two sons.

'It is easier to incite good and decent people to kill when their target is not human but a demon,' said defence attorney Paul Weinberg. 'Kristen Gilbert is not a monster, she is a human being.'

This won little sympathy from the relatives of the victims.

Claire Jagadowski, widow of 66-year-old Stanley Jagadowski, told the judge: 'I still listen for his key in the door. Now I have to face old age alone.'

Gilbert herself declined to take the stand and wept softly when the decision was handed down.

After six hours' deliberation, the jury decided against the death penalty, though the decision was not unanimous. Instead, the judge sentenced her to four consecutive terms of life imprisonment without possibility of parole, plus 20 years. There was no audible reaction in the courtroom. Her parents wept and the victims' families sat stone-faced.

'It's a very bittersweet day when you think your daughter is going to get life imprisonment instead of the death penalty,' said Gilbert's father, Richard Strickland.

Gilbert dropped her appeal after the US Supreme Court ruled that she risked the death penalty on retrial. Her life sentence would be served at the Carswell Federal Medical Center in Fort Worth, Texas.

CHAPTER 12

AMELIA DYER

AT 11 A.M. ON THE MORNING OF 30 MARCH 1896, William Povey was walking along the riverbank at Sonning, where the River Kennet joins the Thames near Reading, when he saw a woman carrying a brown paper parcel tucked under her cloak. Later, he saw the woman returning without the parcel. A bargeman named Charles Humphreys then spotted a brown paper parcel floating in shallow water.

When he caught hold of it with his punt-hook to pull it into his boat, the wet paper tore and a baby's leg stuck out. He reported his find to the police, who came to collect it.

Dr William Maurice opened the parcel in the mortuary and found it contained the body of a baby girl with a white tape knotted around her neck and a brick.

The paper wrapped around the child's body had on it a label from Bristol Temple Meads railway station and a name and address: 'Mrs Thomas, 26 Piggott's Road, Lower Caversham.'

A clerk at the station confirmed that a parcel had been delivered to Mrs Thomas at 26 Piggott's Road, but she had since moved to

45 Kensington Road in nearby Reading, where she was living as Mrs Harding.

Baby Doris's fate

Meanwhile, an advertisement had appeared in the *Bristol Times and Mirror*. It read: 'MARRIED couple with no family would adopt healthy child, nice country home. Terms, £10 – Harding, care of Ship's Letter Exchange, Stokes Croft, Bristol.'

Alongside it was another small advertisement that read: 'NURSE CHILD – Wanted, respectable woman to take young child at home – State terms to Mrs. Scott, 23 Manchester Street, Cheltenham.'

Mrs Scott was, in fact, 23-year-old barmaid Evelina Edith Marmon, a single mother who was not in a position to support her three-month-old baby daughter, Doris.

She hoped to find someone to take care of her child for a weekly fee in the hope that, if her circumstances changed, she could reclaim her later.

During the Victorian era 'baby farming' was a common phenomenon. Unmarried women risked ruin if they had a child, so others would take them in, either for a regular stipend or a flat fee. Unfortunately, those who took a flat fee had little incentive to spend money on their wards and some simply killed off the children in their care as soon as the fee was paid.

Evelina exchanged letters with Mrs Harding, who assured her: 'Myself and my husband are dearly fond of children. I have no child of my own. A child with me will have a good home and a mother's love and care. We belong to the Church of England.' In fact, Mrs Harding, whose real name was Amelia Dyer, had long separated from her husband and had two children – a son and a daughter – of her own. She said she would take baby Doris for a flat fee of £10 (worth an estimated £1,300/$1,700 today). There would be no further expenses.

The day after the body of the baby girl had been fished from the Thames, Mrs Dyer went to Cheltenham to collect Doris, along with her baby clothes, which were packed in a carpetbag. She took the £10 and assured Evelina that she could visit Doris whenever she wished.

From there, Dyer took Doris on the train to Paddington, arriving at 9 p.m. She then took the omnibus to 76 Mayo Road, Willesden, where her daughter Mary Ann – known as Polly – lived with her husband Alfred Palmer. A woman named Ann Beattie offered to carry the carpetbag for her. She saw a young woman waiting by the door. Inside, Dyer knotted a white ribbon around Doris's neck and strangled her.

'Dear little boy' strangled

Mrs Harding's small ad also appeared in the *Weekly Despatch*, where it was seen by Amelia Sargeant, an undertaker's wife who had six children of her own. She was also caring for 13-month-old Harry Simmonds for six shillings (30p, the equivalent of £38/$50 now) a week. However, his mother had wanted Harry to be adopted. Mrs Sargeant found keeping him a struggle so Mrs Harding's advertisement seemed to be the answer.

She replied to the advertisement and got an answer from Mrs Harding, at 45 Kensington Road, Reading, saying she would be happy to take the 'dear little boy'.

'I have no child of my own,' she said. 'He would be well brought up and have a mother's love and care.'

In further correspondence, Mrs Harding said she was actually Mrs Thomas, but did not want to advertise under her own name. Mrs Sargeant visited 45 Kensington Road, which was clean and comfortable, and she agreed that Mrs Thomas should have the child for a flat fee. However, she was not to bring him to Reading. Instead, the handover should take place at Paddington Station.

The day after Mrs Dyer had turned up with Doris, she and a woman she said was her niece met Mrs Sargeant and her husband at Paddington. They were accompanied by a child named Harold. Mrs Sargeant handed over Harry, along with £5, and said the remaining £5 would be paid in ten days' time. She also said she would send Harry's clothes when she got home.

Back at Mayo Road, Mrs Dyer put Harold to bed, but when he began to cry Mrs Dyer strangled him too. That evening, seemingly without a care in the world, she went with her daughter and son-in-law to see the Sporting and Military Show at Olympia. The Palmers slept soundly that night and Mrs Dyer settled down again on the couch, but in the small hours she was awoken by what she thought was the sound of a baby crying. Checking under the couch she found that the two small packages containing the dead children were quite still.

The following afternoon, Mrs Dyer packed the two little bundles into a carpetbag, adding two bricks from the next-door neighbour's garden. Her daughter and son-in-law accompanied her to Paddington, where she caught the 9.15 p.m. train to Reading, arriving there at 10.05 p.m. It was raining as she lugged the heavy bag down the dark streets to the river. After she had made sure there was nobody about, she dropped the bag into the water from the Clappers footbridge. As she hurried home, she was spotted by John Toller, an engineer from Reading Gaol. He said she was empty-handed.

Decomposing body in cupboard

The police investigating the baby's body found in the river discovered that Mrs Harding was in the business of adopting children, so they sent a young woman to 45 Kensington Road. Mrs Harding was not there, but she was greeted by an old lady who identified herself as

'Granny Smith'. She told the young woman to come back two days later. When she returned, Mrs Harding agreed to adopt a child, which she should bring 'tomorrow evening after dark'. Instead, Detective Sergeant Harry James and Constable James Anderson arrived at the front door. They showed Mrs Harding the brown paper that had wrapped the baby's body, which bore her name and previous address, but she could offer no explanation. She claimed that she had received a package when she was living at Caversham and had put the wrapping paper in the bin with the rest of the rubbish.

Under questioning, Mrs Harding revealed that her real name was Dyer, though she sometimes used the name Thomas, which was the surname of her first husband. A search of the house revealed piles of babywear, pawn tickets for children's clothing which had not been redeemed and correspondence concerning the adoption of children for money. Far worse, a stench coming from a cupboard indicated that a body had been left there to decompose before being disposed of. Then in a sewing basket the police found white tape, similar to that found around the neck of the child fished from the Thames, and macramé string like that tied around the parcel.

Dyer was then arrested and at the police station she produced a small pair of scissors and tried to harm herself. They had to be wrested from her. She then tried to strangle herself with a lace from her boots.

The amount of children's clothing found in Dyer's house indicated that there were probably other victims, so the police set about dragging the river. They found the bodies of seven children, but only two could be identified. They were those of Doris Marmon and Harry Simmonds, who were identified by Evelina Marmon and Amelia Sargeant.

Confessing, Dyer said: 'You'll know mine by the tape around their necks.'

Gaol confession

Dyer was then charged with the murder of the children. The police also visited Mayo Road, where the bricks used to weigh down the bag were identified by the Palmers' landlord, who had been moving a fire grate. Arthur Palmer and Polly were charged as accomplices, but Dyer made a confession from Reading Gaol, exonerating them. Addressed to Superintendent Tewsley and dated 16 April 1896, it read, with spelling and punctuation as the original:

> Sir will you kindly grant me the favour of presenting this to the magistrates on Satturday the 18th instant I have made this statement out, for I may not have the oportunity then I must releive my mind I do know and I feel my days are numbered on this earth but I do feel it is an awful thing drawing innocent people into trouble I do know I shal have to answer before my Maker in Heaven for the awful crimes I have committed but as God Almighty is my judge in Heaven as on Hearth neither my daughter Mary Ann Palmer nor her husband Alfred Ernest Palmer I do most solemnly declare neither of them had any thing at all to do with it, they never knew I contemplated doing such a wicked thing until it was to late I am speaking the truth and nothing but the truth as I hope to be forgiven, I myself and I alone must stand before my Maker in Heaven to give a answer for it all witnes my hand Amelia Dyer.

Long career as baby farmer

Although charged with only two murders, Amelia Dyer had been in the baby-farming business for nearly 30 years. Born Amelia Hobley in Pyle Marsh, near Bristol in 1838, she had received a good education and served an apprenticeship as a corset maker. At 24 she married 57-year-old George Thomas and had to give up training as a nurse when she gave birth to a son. She also met midwife Ellen Dane, who took in unmarried pregnant women and worked as a baby farmer.

At the age of 31, Mrs Thomas found herself widowed. After farming out her own child, she went into baby farming on her own account, under the name of Mrs Harding. Then in 1872 she married William Dyer, an unskilled labourer. The following year, they had a daughter named Mary Ann, aka Polly. When her husband lost his job, Mrs Dyer went back into the baby-farming business. She offered a 'premium' service, which meant that after a one-off payment the mother would not be seeing the child again.

Women came to Dyer's house to give birth and numerous babies in her care were registered as 'stillborn'. One doctor became suspicious when the deaths of four infants were registered in two weeks. One of them was three-month-old May Walters, who died of malnutrition, weighing just 6½ lb (3 kg). However, escaping prosecution for murder on a technicality, she was sentenced to six months' hard labour for causing death by neglect.

She then tried other trades but after moving house she went back into baby farming. One baby she took in was the child of a governess whose father was the son of her employer, which would normally have made marriage out of the question. The mother paid Dyer £15 to have the baby adopted, but after a few weeks she turned up to ensure that the child was being well cared for, only to be shown another infant which did not have her baby's distinctive birthmark.

When the mother demanded her baby back, Dyer evaded the issue by cutting her throat in a failed suicide bid and was sent to an insane asylum. When she was released, she moved and continued baby farming. By this time the family had relented and the couple had married, so they tracked down Dyer in search of their child. This time, Dyer attempted to overdose on laudanum, attacking a doctor who came to her aid with a poker. After another spell in the asylum, she tried drowning herself and was returned to the same institution. However, little could be found wrong with her, so she was sent to the workhouse.

Mystery of floating parcel solved

There she met Jane 'Granny' Smith, a penniless widow who had lost her children as well as her husband. They went into baby farming together, though they were forced to move when the newly formed National Society for the Prevention of Cruelty to Children took an interest. Smith did not seem to be puzzled when children suddenly went missing, having been found a 'good home', and nor was she surprised by the large amount of children's clothes that were pawned and never redeemed.

One of the children they took in was nine-year-old Willie Thornton, who brought with him an old carpetbag which he later identified as the bag containing the bodies of Doris Marmon and Harry Simmonds. For a while Arthur and Polly Palmer lived with them in Caversham, before Dyer, Smith and Willie moved to Reading and the Palmers moved to Willesden.

An advertisement in the *Western Daily Express* under the name 'Mrs Thornley' drew a response from May Fry, who had recently given birth to Helena. Thornley – that is, Dyer – agreed to take the child for £10 and collected her from Bristol Temple Meads station. At around 9 p.m., Dyer returned home with a brown paper parcel about two feet long and about a week later Smith noticed a bad smell coming from a cupboard. Soon afterwards, Dyer left the house with a brown paper parcel, saying she was going to pawn the contents.

The parcel contained the remains of Helena Fry, the baby discovered by Charles Humphreys, the bargeman. Her tragic end would be the key to unmasking a monster.

Found guilty and executed

At the Old Bailey, Dyer confessed to the murder of Helena Fry, along with those of Doris Marmon and Harry Simmonds, but pleaded insanity. This plea was dismissed and it took the jury less than five minutes to return a guilty verdict. She was hanged at Newgate Prison on 10 June 1897. The case gave a welcome boost to the NSPCC and the laws concerning adoption were tightened. Over her long career, Dyer may have killed as many as 300–400 children, making her one of the most prolific serial killers in history.

Arthur Palmer then appeared in court but was discharged. Later he was convicted of deserting a four-year-old girl in Devonport, where he and Polly were living under the name of Mr and Mrs Paton. Polly was to appear at a separate trial at the Berkshire Assizes in Reading and her lawyer took out a subpoena for Mrs Dyer to appear as a witness. However, the date of the hearing fell after her execution and the Home Secretary decided that the execution could not be delayed. He declared that the law must run its course and that Dyer was 'legally dead' from the time the death sentence had been pronounced. No evidence was presented at the assizes and Polly walked free.

Two years later, a three-week-old baby girl was found wrapped in a parcel under the seat of a railway carriage in a siding in Newton Abbot. The child was alive and had recently been adopted by a 'Mrs Stewart'. When Mrs Stewart was arrested, she turned out to be Dyer's daughter Polly.

CHAPTER 13

CHELSEA O'MAHONEY

CHELSEA O'MAHONEY WAS just 14 years old when she killed. In some ways, she can also be seen as a victim – though the *Sunday Times* called her a 'natural-born teenage killer' while the London *Evening Standard* said she 'killed for kicks' in a brutal 'happy slapping' attack.

Heroin-addicted mother

Chelsea Kayleigh Peaches O'Mahoney was born at Edgware Hospital on 15 November 1989. She was the daughter of Susanne Cato, a heroin addict, who had known Chelsea's father only casually. A fellow addict, he was in jail when his daughter was born and little more is known of him.

Cato, who already had two children and went on to have two more, used to inject heroin in front of her daughter. Witnesses recalled seeing blood spurting on to the walls and the floor. She was also a heavy drinker and Chelsea would wade through discarded bottles, scavenging for food. Severely neglected as an infant, she was found wandering the streets alone at night at the age of three.

At seven, the local authority, the London Borough of Barnet, intervened. They placed her with an uncle and aunt in south London, who had no children of their own but had passed the same strict tests required of unrelated foster carers. The court restricted contact between Chelsea and her mother to conversations on the telephone, but Cato frequently promised to phone, then didn't, or else she would call under the influence of drink and drugs. Either way, the result was to upset Chelsea and in 1998 telephone communication was terminated with Chelsea's agreement.

Member of gang

Otherwise, Chelsea responded well to her new, more stable, environment. At school, she was found to be intelligent and particularly enjoyed art. Teachers were optimistic about her progress. But at home, she was often withdrawn. While generally well behaved, Chelsea showed an inability to communicate with those around her. There were also occasional emotional outbursts which her uncle and aunt found difficult to cope with.

They tried family therapy and when that failed Chelsea was fostered by another aunt, who lived nearby on the Ethelred Estate in Kennington. There Chelsea mixed with older boys, playing football with Reece Sargeant, Darren Case and David Blenman, with whom she later had a relationship. He too had not known his father, and his mother's care had been sporadic, so he was mainly brought up by an aunt and his grandmother. His attendance at school was poor and when he was there he was violent and disruptive.

In an attempt to straighten him out, he was sent to live with relatives in Barbados but it did no good. After he returned to London, he built up a long list of convictions for petty crime and affray. He was a natural-born gangster and although he was four years younger than Sargeant and a year younger than Case, he dominated them. However, the lynchpin of the gang was O'Mahoney, who was one year his junior.

Able student

When her aunt became seriously ill, Chelsea had to be moved again, this time to an unrelated couple who had fostered successfully before. The new arrangement seemed promising as Chelsea's new family had indicated that they would like to keep her until she was 18. They lived in South Norwood, so Chelsea could stay on at Norwood School, then a girls' comprehensive. Teachers complained that she was occasionally late and sometimes impertinent, but after the school wrote to her foster parents her attendance and behaviour improved. Generally, Chelsea was regarded as an able student who loved reading. She did not like talking about herself, but in one-to-one situations she could be thoughtful and compassionate. At least one teacher received a Christmas card from her.

Nights of crime and violence

However, there was one issue that made her foster parents seek advice from social services. Chelsea had asked to stay overnight with friends. Was that okay? Social workers advised the foster carers to determine the issue as if she were their own daughter. Chelsea finally convinced them that she was having a sleepover with a girlfriend. Satisfied that she would be staying in an appropriate environment, her foster parents allowed it.

But Chelsea had lied. Instead of visiting a girlfriend, she was out with Blenman, Sargeant and Case, drinking and planning 'ramping', or street robberies. These were recorded in her diary. One entry read: 'Whats goin on I just came home yesterday I had an all nighter with Barry, Darren and Reece. I was Jokers or we went bare places. I was happy all right because Barry kept ramping all the time.'

Worse than that, random violence was involved: 'Them lot bang up some old homeless man which I fink is bad, even doe I woz laughen after.' The violence did not put her off, though. She just wanted to remain part of the gang. Together they smoked weed and were obsessed with graffiti.

During their all-nighters, the gang would move out of Kennington towards inner London. This was an easier hunting ground because even streetwise Londoners let their guard down on the busy and well-lit streets there. They would snatch peoples' mobile phones or mug them, punching victims and kicking them on the ground. Chelsea began filming these attacks on her smartphone.

First victim on fatal night

On the evening of 29 October 2004, Chelsea left her neat bedroom in South Norwood for another all-nighter with the gang. Bored with Kennington, Blenman led the gang to the South Bank for a 50-minute reign of terror that would be recorded on CCTV there.

Their first victim was 24-year-old actor David Dobson, who had been working as a barman in the Old Vic theatre. He was heading down Lower Marsh on his way home when the way ahead was blocked by a gang of hoodies. There were two black boys, a white boy and a white girl. The girl was carrying a blue bag and all of them were wearing hooded tops.

The tallest of the boys approached him and asked him the time. Before he could answer, he had been punched in the face. Once on the ground he was kicked repeatedly, but he managed to scramble to his feet and make off. The gang did not chase after him and he escaped. This was the first of eight assaults and not once did the gang run. They simply strolled from attack to attack.

When they turned towards the river they came across Alistair Whiteside and his friend David Morley, bar manager at the Admiral

Duncan in Old Compton Street, a Soho gay bar. He had survived the nail-bomb attack there by neo-Nazi David Copeland on 30 April 1999, which had killed three people and left Morley permanently deaf in the left ear.

Kicked dying man's head

Five years on, Morley and Whiteside had finished work in Soho at around 3 a.m. and had taken the 15-minute walk across the river to the South Bank. They were sitting on a bench near Hungerford Bridge when the gang spotted them. The girl, later identified as O'Mahoney, approached them with an amused look on her face and her camera phone in her hand, saying: 'We're doing a documentary on happy slapping. Pose for the camera.'

While she filmed, the two men were pulled from the bench and beaten savagely. Whitehead got off more lightly than Morley. He watched while his friend was stamped and jumped on, O'Mahoney joining in enthusiastically.

When the violence subsided, O'Mahoney picked up the bags and belongings of the two men, including Whitehead's mobile phone. Then Whitehead said he saw her kick Morley's head like 'a footballer taking a penalty'. She then checked her phone and walked quietly away to join the others.

Morley was taken to hospital where he was operated on, but he died in intensive care. Five of his ribs were broken and he had suffered a ruptured spleen. The pathologist would count 44 separate injuries, likening his condition to that of a car crash victim or someone who had fallen from a great height.

Further violence

The gang went on to attack three foreign-exchange students, stealing a mobile phone and a bottle of beer from them before sauntering

The gang – clockwise from top left: Reece Sargeant, Darren Case, David Blenman and Chelsea O'Mahoney.

on to Jubilee Gardens at the back of the London Eye. Nigel Elliot, who had missed his train, was sitting on a bench there, gathering his thoughts when, suddenly, the bottle stolen from the student was smashed over his head. His pockets were then rifled. When he tried to get to his feet and run he was tripped up and at least two attackers kicked him in the face.

They wandered on to find a homeless man named Wayne Miller sleeping in an underpass. He was awoken at around 3.30 a.m. by a savage kick in the back. A CCTV recording showed Blenman, Sargeant and Case savagely beating him, while O'Mahoney filmed them. One of his attackers put his hands against the wall to support himself while he jumped on Miller with both feet.

The gang then calmly walked away and headed back to Kennington. Miller escaped serious injury, but Morley was dying while the gang members reviewed the footage of their savagery, particularly relishing their victims' pleas for mercy. Sargeant called his girlfriend at 4 a.m., boasting that he was speaking to her on a stolen phone.

Apprehended by police

The police investigating the death of David Morley at first thought it was a homophobic attack, but soon it became clear that the gang had attacked people indiscriminately. With gang members using the mobile phones they had stolen, tracking them down was easy. Added to that, informants were plentiful. One 15-year-old friend of O'Mahoney's said she had heard the gang talking about targeting 'tramps, druggies and just people on the street' two days before the attack. They had also discussed how to divide the spoils.

A week after Morley died, the police were outside Chelsea's foster parents' home when they saw her enter carrying the same blue bag that is clearly visible in CCTV footage of the attacks. She was also wearing a hoodie. Without prompting she told officers: 'That's what I wore on the night.'

In her bedroom, they found her diary detailing previous attacks. However, she had wiped the incriminating footage from her mobile phone and denied filming the incidents, saying she was merely looking through the phonebook. She claimed that she was just an innocent spectator and asked: 'What was I supposed to do? Now if I'd tried to stop them, what if they'd like . . . what if they'd have turned on me like, what was I supposed to do?'

Trial and sentencing

Chelsea O'Mahoney was 16 in January 2006, when she was convicted of manslaughter and conspiracy to cause grievous bodily harm along with Reece Sargeant, 21, Darren Case, 18, and David Blenman, 17. She held hands with a social worker during the trial. O'Mahoney was sentenced to eight years in jail, while the three men were given 12 years each. What she had not expected was to be named and shamed by the judge as she was still a minor.

Mr Justice Barker told her at the Old Bailey: 'You became obsessed with the activity of catching people unawares, assaulting them and then filming it for your later gratification. . . . You called this "happy slapping" – no victim on the receiving end would dignify it with such a deceptive description. You sought enjoyment from humiliation and pleasure from the infliction of pain.'

Refusing an appeal, Lord Justice Gage said the killing came 'very close to the top of the scale in the range of seriousness' for offences of manslaughter.

While detained at Oakhill Secure Training Centre in Milton Keynes, she complained of being restrained by the prison officers. She was released in 2010 after serving just four years and the *Sun* tracked her to a probation hostel in Bedford, where she was seen laughing and joking with friends while on a shopping trip. Asked if she thought justice had been done, she said: 'I don't know what you are talking about.'

Geoffrey Morley, then 81, who with his wife Doreen had adopted David as a child, said: 'These people did some terrible things. My wife and I didn't speak about the case while it was happening and want to remain quiet about it. I hope Chelsea O'Mahoney can find a new bunch of friends and start rebuilding her life.'

CHAPTER 14

EDITH THOMPSON

AROUND MIDNIGHT ON 3 October 1922, Edith Thompson and her husband Percy were walking back to their home at 41 Kensington Gardens, Ilford, after an evening at the Criterion Theatre in London's West End. As they approached their front door a man leapt from the shadows, knocking Edith to the ground. He then stabbed her husband, thrusting the knife into Percy's mouth and cutting one of the carotid arteries that carry blood to the brain.

At first dazed, Edith cried out: 'Oh don't! Oh don't!'

The attacker fled and as he passed under the street light she saw he was wearing a blue overcoat and a grey trilby hat. Edith said she then noticed blood pouring from her husband's mouth and she ran to fetch help. Meeting neighbours Percy Cleveley and Dora Pittard, she screamed: 'Oh my God, will you help me? My husband is ill. He is bleeding.'

The three of them ran to the nearby doctor's surgery. Edith rang the bell and dashed back to her husband, leaving Miss Pittard to explain the situation. Asked what had happened, Edith said: 'Don't ask me. I don't know. Somebody flew past, and when I turned to speak to him blood was pouring out of his mouth. Then he fell down.' By the time Dr Noel Maudsley arrived at the scene a few minutes later, Mr Thompson was dead.

'Why did you not come sooner and save him?' said Edith.

Later she told Percy's brother Richard that Percy had been walking along when he 'suddenly came over queer, fell against the wall and slid down saying, "Oh"'. She claimed that he had been complaining about pains in his legs on the way from the station and the doctor had said he died from a haemorrhage.

Initially, she told the police the same thing – that her husband had suddenly dropped down and screamed out. She said she was not carrying a knife, nor was her husband. Asked if she or her husband had seen or spoken to anybody, she said she had not noticed anyone. When they wanted to know how she accounted for the cuts to his neck, she said he had fallen against the wall.

The Criterion Theatre as it is today.

Bywaters held by the police

However, it was clear to the police that Percy had been murdered, so they began looking for a motive. Richard Thompson told them that a sailor who had been lodging with them was 'overly familiar' with his brother's wife. His name was Frederick Bywaters. Things came to a head when Bywaters intervened in an argument between Percy and Edith, during which Percy hit his wife. Percy then ordered Bywaters out of the house.

On the night of the murder Bywaters visited Edith's parents' house in nearby Manor Park, leaving at 11 p.m. He returned to his mother's house in Upper Norwood at 3 a.m. the following morning. At 6.15 p.m., he called at Edith's parents' house again, saying he was leaving on the passenger liner *Morea* from Tilbury on the following day. Edith's father, William Graydon, then showed him a story in the *Evening News* about the murder and told him that Edith was being held at Ilford Police Station. A few minutes later, the police arrived.

At Ilford Police Station, Bywaters said he knew nothing about Percy Thompson's murder except what he had read in the newspaper. He said he did not have a knife, but admitted that he might have received letters from Mrs Thompson. The police then found some in his bedroom.

Edith's statement

Edith Thompson also made a statement, saying:

> I know Freddie Bywaters . . . We have been in the habit of corresponding with one another. His letters to me and mine to him were couched in affectionate terms. I am not in possession of any letters he writes to me. I have destroyed all as is customary with me with all my correspondence. The letters shown to me by Inspector Hall and addressed to Mr F.

Bywaters are some of the letters that I wrote to Freddie, and were written to him without my husband's consent. When he was at home in England, we were in the habit of going out occasionally together without my husband's knowledge.

When Inspector Hall escorted Edith out of the interview room, he led her past the library where Bywaters was being held. Seeing him, she said: 'Oh, God! Oh, God, what can I do? Why did he do it? I did not want him to do it.' Then she added: 'I must tell the truth.'

Inspector Hall said: 'You realize what you are saying; what you might say may be used in evidence.'

She then made a second statement, saying:

When we got near Endsleigh Gardens a man rushed out from the gardens and knocked me away and pushed me away from my husband. I was dazed for a moment. When I recovered I saw my husband scuffling with a man. The man whom I know as Freddie Bywaters was running away. He was wearing a blue overcoat and a grey hat. I know it was him although I did not see his face.

Bywaters accepts responsibility

Bywaters was shown Edith's statement and was told they were both going to be charged with murder. He then made another statement, saying:

Mrs Edith Thompson was not aware of my movements on Tuesday night, 3rd October. I left Manor Park at 11 p.m. and proceeded to Ilford. I waited for Mrs Thompson and her husband. When near Endsleigh Gardens I pushed her to one side, also pushing him further up the street. I said to him, 'You have got to separate from your wife.' He said, 'No.' I said, 'You will have to.' We struggled, I took my knife from my pocket and we fought and he got the worst of it. Mrs Thompson must have been spellbound for I saw nothing of her during the fight. I ran away through Endsleigh Gardens . . . The reason I fought with Thompson was because he never acted like a man to his wife. He always seemed several degrees lower than a snake. I loved her and I could not go on seeing her leading that life. I did not intend to kill him. I only meant to injure him. I gave him an opportunity of standing up to me as a man but he wouldn't. I have had the knife some time. It was a sheath knife. I threw it down a drain when I was running through Endsleigh Gardens.

The knife was recovered four days later. At the time there was insufficient evidence to charge Edith Thompson. However, in Bywaters' box on board the *Morea* the police found more of her letters and also newspaper cuttings that incriminated her.

Beginning of affair

Edith had been born Edith Graydon in Dalston in 1893. Frederick Bywaters' parents moved there in 1902, a few months before he was born, and later he attended the same school as her younger brothers. When she was 14 she met 19-year-old Percy Thompson, who assured her father that he would do the right thing by her. He would not 'get her into trouble' and would wait until she was old enough to marry. They did so in 1916 and moved to Ilford. Meanwhile, Bywaters had joined the merchant navy and gone to sea.

When his ship was being refitted in Tilbury, in 1920, he moved in with the Graydons as a lodger. There he renewed his acquaintanceship with Edith and was introduced to Percy when he and Edith came to dine on Fridays. In June 1921 the Thompsons took a holiday on the Isle of Wight and invited Freddie and Edith's younger sister Avis, a matchmaking attempt that did not work. Instead, Bywaters and Edith shared a kiss on a charabanc trip. Afterwards, Bywaters moved into the Thompsons' house in Kensington Gardens as a lodger.

On 27 June, Freddie's birthday, Edith took him breakfast in bed while Percy was at work and then, as a special birthday present, she joined him between the sheets. The affair continued under her husband's nose until October, when Bywaters went back to sea. She wrote to him, saying: 'We've said we'll always be pals, haven't we? Shall we say we'll always be lovers even tho' secret ones, or is it (this great big love) a thing we can't control?'

When Freddie came back from sea, Percy could not help but notice that something was going on between his wife and Bywaters. This provoked a row between Edith and her husband. He hit her and a chair was knocked over. At that point, Bywaters intervened and Percy told him to leave the house, though Edith maintained that her husband and Bywaters were friends again before Freddie left.

Edith's letters

Edith kept on seeing Bywaters and when he went back to sea she continued writing to him, telling him of her sexual revulsion for her husband and speculating about killing him. Percy was being treated for insomnia and she said she had tried to find the sleeping draught he had been prescribed, so she could give him an overdose. 'It would be so easy, darling,' she wrote.

She also sent him newspaper cuttings about murders. One concerned Dr Preston Wallis, who lodged with the Reverend Horace Bolding and his young wife Ada. Bolding was found dead, poisoned with hyoscine, after a relationship developed between Ada and Wallis.

Frederick Bywaters (left), Edith Thompson (centre) and Percy Thompson (right) in July 1921.

Her letters contained a quote from Robert Hichens' novel *Bella Donna*: 'It must be remembered that digitalin is a cumulative poison and that the same dose is harmless if taken once, yet frequently repeated, becomes deadly.' She went on to say: 'Is it any use?'

Then there was a cutting about the dancer Freda Kempton, who died of an overdose of cocaine, which 'may be interesting'; and another about a murder case where chicken broth was laced with rat poison. They discussed putting a lethal dose of quinine in Percy's tea, though he would be sure to taste it, it was thought. Instead, she said she would feed him glass from a broken light bulb.

'I used the light bulb three times, but the third time he found a piece so I have given it up until you come home,' she wrote.

She also played on Bywaters' feelings, saying: 'Yes, darling, you are jealous of him but I want you to be. He has the right by law to all that you have the right to by nature and love. Yes, darling, be jealous, so much that you will do something desperate.'

While these letters implicated Edith in the murder, when a post-mortem was conducted by the noted forensic pathologist Bernard Spilsbury no glass was found in the intestine and there was no evidence of poisoning.

Bywaters takes the stand

There were queues outside the Old Bailey when the case came to trial that December, with tickets to the public gallery changing hands for £1 – worth perhaps £60/$80 today. The letters and cuttings Edith had sent Bywaters were introduced in evidence, with the prosecution alleging that if there was not an actual conspiracy between them, Mrs Thompson abetted the murder as it was 'incited and directed by her controlling hand'.

'Bywaters committed the murder,' the solicitor-general told the jury, 'then it will be my duty to ask you, after hearing the evidence, to find her who incited and proposed the murder as guilty as Bywaters who committed it.'

Bywaters denied being influenced by Edith's letters. He did not believe that she had tried to poison her husband but thought she was just letting her imagination run riot. Their intention, he said, was merely to obtain a separation and go abroad.

'She mentioned Bombay, Australia, Marseilles,' he said.

Bywaters admitted buying the knife in the previous year and he also had lunch with Edith on the day of the murder, so she was au fait with their plans. However, he had no intention of going to Ilford that night. The impulse seized him suddenly. When he got there, he saw them walking down the road.

I overtook them and pushed Mrs Thompson with my right hand. With my left hand I held Thompson, and caught him by the back of his coat and pushed him along the street, swinging him round. After I swung him round I said to him, 'Why don't you get a divorce or separation, you cad?' He said, 'I know that is what you want, but I am not going to give it you, it would make it too pleasant for both of you.' I said, 'You take a delight in making Edith's life a hell.' Then he said, 'I've got her. I'll keep her, and I'll shoot you.'

Asked why he drew his knife, Bywaters said: 'I thought he was going to shoot me if he had an opportunity, and I tried to stop him.'

This was the first time Bywaters had mentioned that he thought Thompson had a gun, though he admitted he did not see one.

When it was pointed out that he had not told the truth in statements he made to the police, Bywaters said: 'Yes, because I wanted to help Mrs Thompson. My one idea was to shield her.'

Edith advised not to testify

Edith's barrister, Sir Henry Curtis-Bennett, advised her not to take the stand. The prosecution case against her only consisted of letters and cuttings and he believed he had 'an answer to every incrimination passage'. However, she insisted and it was her undoing.

In the witness box, she came across as arrogant and showed no contrition over the death of her husband or her infidelity. She denied trying to poison her husband, or trying to feed him glass. Indeed, she said she had entered into a suicide pact with Bywaters as 'it was far easier to be dead'. She insisted that Bywaters had never suggested that he would stab her husband and claimed she had no idea that an attack would be made that night.

Ask why she told the police she had not seen anyone, she said: 'I was very agitated and did not want to say anything against Mr Bywaters. I wanted to shield him.'

However, she said that the idea of putting something in her husband's food to make him ill and perhaps give him a heart attack was Bywaters'. She had humoured him by pretending that she wanted to kill her husband.

Bywaters' counsel, Cecil Whitely, did not challenge this and he and his colleague did not take the opportunity to cross-examine Mrs Thompson. Whitely pointed out that:

> the poignant tragedy so far as Bywaters is concerned, is that there is sitting next to him in that box one who is charged jointly with him, one who is dearer to him than his own life . . . My instructions, and those given to my learned friend, were that neither by word nor deed, in conducting this case on behalf of this man, should a word be said by us, or any action taken by us, which would in any way hamper the defence of Mrs Thompson.

Nevertheless, Whitely insisted that the letters showed that Bywaters was trying to 'break away from the entanglement' while Mrs Thompson was 'determined that it should not be so'.

In his summing up, the judge, Mr Justice Shearman, said:

> If a woman says to a man, 'I want this man murdered, you promise to do it,' and he then promises her – she believing that he is going to keep his promise as soon as he gets an opportunity – and goes out and murders someone, he is guilty of murder. She is just as much guilty of murder . . .

Both sentenced to death

After two and a quarter hours' deliberation, the jury found them both guilty. Asked if he had anything to say before sentencing, Bywaters said: 'The verdict of the jury is wrong. Edith Thompson is not guilty. I am no murderer. I am not an assassin.'

Edith too insisted she was not guilty. Nevertheless, the judge reached for his black cap and passed a death sentence on them both.

Bywaters then wrote to the Home Secretary, who rejected any plea of mitigation. When Edith heard this, she had to be tied to her bed and sedated. Although during the trial the couple were condemned for their adultery, as they faced death a petition for them to be spared was signed by nearly a million people.

While Bywaters was adjudged admirable for staying loyal to Edith, his mother wrote to the king saying that he had 'fallen under the spell of a woman many years older than himself'. It did no good. Bywaters 'died like a gentleman' in Pentonville Prison at 9 a.m. on 9 January 1923. Edith Thompson was hanged at the same time, half a mile away in Holloway, in a state of collapse. It was said that her 'insides fell out' – leading people to believe that she was pregnant. However, she had been in custody for three months and any pregnancy would have been apparent. In that case, the execution would have been stayed and she would almost certainly have been spared. In order to prevent such a thing happening again, all women who were hanged after that date were made to wear a special canvas garment.

CHAPTER 15

SUSAN NEWELL

AT ABOUT 8 A.M. on 21 June 1923, lorry driver Thomas Dickson saw a woman and a young girl struggling with a heavily laden handcart in Coatbridge, Lanarkshire. As he approached, the woman cried out: 'Are you going to Glasgow?' He was, so he stopped and gave them a lift.

The woman said she was going to Glasgow to look for a place to live. When they got there, he dropped them off on Duke Street. As he helped her get her handcart down off the lorry, he noticed that she was anxious to avoid disturbing the bed mat that was covering a bundle. When he tried to steady the bundle, she knocked his hand away.

Mrs Helen Elliot was looking out of her kitchen window in a nearby house when she saw a little foot, then a head, pop out from under the bed mat. The woman tried to secure them with a rag. By then, Mrs Elliot had gone downstairs to collect her sister Mary and the two of them went outside. The woman was again trying to cover the bundle, this time with a brown coat, but it was too late.

As she made off with the handcart, the two women chased after her. The girl accompanying her took over pushing the cart, while the woman put the bundle on her back. When retired soldier Robert Foote joined the chase, he saw the woman frantically trying to climb a wall, then some railings. He summoned Police Constable McGennett, who was on patrol in the area.

When PC McGennett apprehended the woman, he asked her where the bundle was. She led him to the rolled-up bed mat and when he examined it he found it contained the body of a small boy. Asked if she had anything to say, the woman replied: 'It was not me who did it. It was my husband.'

Newspaper boy murdered

Three weeks earlier, 29-year-old Susan Newell and her husband John had moved into rooms in 2 Newlands Street, Whifflet, Coatbridge. They were always rowing and their landlady, Annie Young, who lived downstairs, gave them notice to quit. In the meantime, Mrs Newell went to the police and complained that her husband had assaulted her. She then told Mrs Young that he beat her six-year-old daughter Janet. On top of that, she also accused her husband of neglect.

He had taken his 30 shillings (£1.50, worth around £81/$107 today) wages and had not left her any housekeeping, she said. She had not seen him since.

On the following day, Wednesday 20 June 1923, Susan's daughter Janet was playing out in the street in the evening when newspaper delivery boy John Johnstone turned up at the Newells' one-room apartment. Mrs Young and two neighbours, Mrs Brown and Mrs Morgan, were in the kitchen below and heard him go up the stairs. Then there were three thuds, which they took to be the sound of Mrs Newell packing, and a few minutes later she came down to the kitchen to ask Mrs Young if she had a box. She hadn't.

At 11 o'clock that night, John Johnstone's father went to the police station to report his 13-year-old son missing. His body was found the next day in Glasgow, in the bundle Mrs Newell had been pushing on the handcart, and he was identified by his father and grandmother.

Accuses husband

A post-mortem was conducted the following day by Professor John Glaister. He gave the cause of death as throttling – compression of the windpipe by hand. This had been done with such force that the boy's spine had been dislocated. There were also marks of the 'forcible application' of a blunt instrument on the head by more than one blow. Signs of burning were also evident, but they were probably caused by the child falling against a lit gas ring.

Mrs Newell claimed that she had had a row with her husband the previous night. He had struck her and the newspaper boy, who was in the house at the time, had screamed. When she told her husband that she was going to lodge a complaint, he grabbed the boy, pushed him on to the bed and choked him until he was black in the face. She then fainted, she said, and when she came to the boy was dead and her husband was gone. Not knowing what to do, she rolled the body up in a mat and lay it on the couch while her daughter went to bed. The following morning, she put the body on the handcart and made for Glasgow.

Visiting the Newells' lodgings, Chief Constable William McDonald and Detective Sergeant Charles Lockhart found the place in 'disorder'. The gas was still burning and the handcart, it turned out, had been borrowed from Mrs Young. There was no doubt that 2 Newlands Street was the scene of the murder.

Questioned by WPCs Blair and Duncan, Janet said that she had seen the boy go into the house. Asked what had happened to him, she said: 'My daddy choked him with his hands and he died.' Her mother, she said, had been standing at the foot of the bed and had told him to stop. Then he had hit Janet with the poker.

John Newell's alibi

John Newell was in Haddington near Edinburgh when he read of the murder and his wife's arrest in *The Scotsman*. He went straight to the police station there and was arrested. When taken back to Coatbridge and cautioned, he said he knew nothing about the murder and was not at home at the time.

He left home at 11.15 a.m. on Tuesday to collect 30 shillings from his work and attend his brother's funeral. Another brother, David, was with him when his wife assaulted him in the street, headbutting him twice in the face. He then visited his father's house before spending the night in the Parkhead Model Lodging House.

He returned to Coatbridge at 10.30 a.m. on Wednesday to buy some liver. After cooking a meal at the lodging house, he went to Glasgow to do some shopping, before going to a pub.

Even though he had been back in Coatbridge that evening, he had not returned home. He went to the music hall, where he had a beer, and then at 10.30 p.m. he visited his sister, Mrs Shanks, in Buchanan Street. After an hour he went to the police station, as there was a warrant out for his arrest on a charge of deserting his wife. However, he was not arrested. He then stayed in a lodging house before heading to Haddington, where he spent another night, as he was intending to leave his wife and move to England. But then he read the newspaper and handed himself in to the police.

Husband and wife on trial

While his alibi checked out, he was still in Coatbridge that Wednesday at the time of the killing, so he was charged with murder and sent for trial alongside his wife at the High Court in Glasgow. A queue for seats in the public gallery began in the middle of the night. Counsel for Susan Newell, T.A. Gentles, objected to every woman selected for the jury, resulting in an all-male panel.

Both defendants pleaded not guilty – John on the strength of his alibi, Susan claiming insanity. The couple sat in the dock with a police officer between them and one more on either side. Dressed in dark clothes, Susan Newell appeared haggard, while her husband wore a suit and clutched his cap in his hands.

Robert Johnstone, the murdered boy's father, said that John had failed to come home after his newspaper round and he thought he had gone to the cinema. However, at 10.30 p.m., when the picture house had closed, he grew more concerned and started searching the streets. Then he reported the matter to the police. The following day, a police officer arrived at his workplace and took him to Glasgow's Eastern Police Station, where he was shown a body. When asked whose body he had seen, he broke down and replied: 'Oh! My boy's body.'

Margaret Johnstone, John's mother, also collapsed in tears when she saw her son's clothing in the courtroom. Mrs Young testified about the Newells' constant rows, but said she had not seen Mr Newell on the day of the murder. She remembered John Johnstone going up to the couple's flat at 6.55 p.m. and then she heard three thumps. After that, she assumed the boy had left, but she had not seen him do so.

Daughter's damning testimony

The star witness was Susan Newell's daughter, six-year-old Janet MacLeod, who was called for the prosecution by Lord Kinross. Previously she had told the police: 'My daddy choked him with his hands and he died.' But in court, she had a different tale to tell.

Questioned gently by Lord Kinross, she said she recalled the boy going up the stairs to her house while she was playing outside, but did not see him come down again. Later, her mammy took her to Duffy's public house, leaving her outside while she had the jug she was carrying filled with beer. She also took home whisky and wine. The implication here was that she had bought the alcohol with money stolen from the paperboy, as her husband had absconded with his wages.

Kinross then asked: 'Where did you go when you got home?'

'Into the room,' Janet replied.

'Did you see anything?'

'A little wee boy dead on the couch.'

'How did you know he was dead?'

'I went over to look.'

'What did your mother say?'

'"Keep quiet."'

'Did your mother do anything?'

'She drank the beer.'

'Did she do anything about the boy?'

'She was trying to get up the floor.'

Apparently, Newell tried to lever up the floorboards so she could hide the boy's body under them.

'Did she touch the boy?' asked Lord Kinross.

'Yes,' replied Janet.

'What did she do?'

'She took my father's drawers and put them over his face. His nose was bleeding. She got a poker to get the floor up to try to get the wee boy in, and we tried to get a box from Mrs Young.'

'The same night, where did you sleep?'

'In the house.'

Janet went on to say that she did not see her stepfather all that day. The day before he had gone to a funeral and he had not come back. Kinross then asked Janet about what she had told WPCs Blair and Duncan – that her daddy had choked the boy with his hands.

'There were two ladies who spoke to you on this happening,' said Kinross, indicating WPCs Blair and Duncan. 'Did you tell them the same as you told us today?'

'No. I forget what I told them,' said Janet.

'Do you remember telling them it was your daddy who choked the boy?'

'Yes.'

'Why did you tell them that?'

'Mammy told me.'

'That is what she told you to say?'

'Yes.'

She admitted that she had not seen the boy harmed though. Then she was questioned about the journey to Glasgow.

'What did you do with the wee laddie?' asked Kinross.

'We put him in a bag. There was a bed mat in it. We went downstairs and I got toffee. There was a go-cart and I got a seat on it.'

'When you sat in it, what did you sit on? The bundle?'

'Yes, on the wee boy.'

Her testimony was damning.

Sanity debate

Lorry driver Thomas Dickson from Airdrie testified about giving Mrs Newell and Janet a lift to Glasgow, and Mrs Elliot of 602 Duke Street, Glasgow, told the court about seeing the foot and head emerge from the bundle. The police also testified that Mrs Newell had said that her husband killed the child.

Witnesses were called to establish John Newell's alibi. The prosecution then withdrew the charges, the jury formally acquitted him and he was discharged. He did not speak to his wife as he left the dock, but she had her eyes fixed on him until he disappeared out of a side exit.

Professor Glaister had been asked by the procurator fiscal to prepare a report on Mrs Newell's sanity, which he submitted on 13 September. Mr Gentles for the defence asked him: 'You have heard evidence that this woman was deserted by her husband, left with no money and about to be turned out on to the street. Is that the kind of thing that might affect her mental balance?'

'It might make her desperate, owing to the cruelty of the situation,' Professor Glaister replied.

Lord Alness, the judge presiding, asked: 'Is there anything in the evidence to suggest that at the time of the crime the woman was suffering from frenzy or insanity?'

'I have heard nothing here nor from her that it existed,' Professor Glaister said.

Mr Gentles then asked: 'I suppose it is possible for a person to be perfectly sane on 13 September who was insane on 20 June?'

'That is so,' said Professor Glaister.

'Have you ever heard of temporary insanity, sudden frenzies, in which a person may have completely lost self-control?'

'Yes, in some cases.'

'What class of society did Mrs Newell come from?'

'Practically of the tinker class.'

'Not a high type mentally or intellectually?'

'No, nor a high moral type.'

Summing up, Mr Gentles pointed out that the 'abnormal condition of mind' Mrs Newell was suffering from justified the reduction of the charge from murder to culpable homicide. There was no evidence of premeditation, nor did she have any malice towards the boy. Taking his body to Glasgow on a handcart was clear evidence of madness, he maintained.

Death by hanging

Lord Alness gave the jury four alternatives. If they found Mrs Newell to be insane, they should acquit. Alternatively, they could return a verdict of 'not proven' under Scottish law. Otherwise they should find her guilty of culpable homicide or murder.

The jury took just 37 minutes to find Susan Newell guilty of murder. She stood motionless in the dock as the judge donned the black cap.

> I decern and adjudge you, Susan Newell, to be carried to the prison of Glasgow, therein to be detained until 10 October, and on that date, within the walls of the prison, and by the hands of the executioner, to be hanged by the neck on the gibbet till you be dead and your body thereafter to be buried within the walls of the prison, and your whole moveable goods are decerned to be escheat and forfeit to His Majesty's use.

She showed no emotion as she stepped down from the dock. The trial had lasted just two days.

No woman had been hanged in Scotland for 50 years and counsel appealed to Lord Novar, Secretary of State for Scotland, for a reprieve. Unfortunately for Newell, earlier that year Edith Thompson had been hanged in England after her lover had killed her husband, and it was decided that the law must be applied evenly on either side of the border.

When Newell was told that her plea for a reprieve had been rejected, she cried out for her daughter and then fainted. However, she had regained her composure when she was sent to the scaffold. She was to be hanged by John Ellis, who had previously hanged Edith Thompson. He hated hanging women, but was known for the speed of his executions.

Newell allowed Ellis to put straps around her waist and thighs but, unwilling to hurt her, he had not pinioned her wrists tightly enough. When he put the white hood over her head, she wriggled her hands free and tore it off, crying: 'Don't put that thing over me.'

Ellis simply pulled the lever and death was instantaneous. Afterwards, he said she was 'very brave'. She would be the last woman to be hanged in Scotland. The execution took place in Duke Street Prison, not far from where she had been arrested, and a crowd of 200, mostly women, held a vigil outside.

Janet was sent to be brought up in a convent, while John Johnstone was honoured by his local community. His school and the local shops closed on the day of his funeral and a huge crowd joined the procession.

CHAPTER 16

CHARLOTTE AND LINDA MULHALL

DUBBED THE SCISSOR SISTERS after the noughties' New York band, Charlotte and Linda Mulhall dismembered their victim in what the judge called 'the most grotesque killing that has occurred in my professional lifetime'.

Like many killers, Charlotte and Linda had a disturbed childhood. Their father, John Mulhall, was a heavy drinker who, in his cups, would beat their mother Kathleen savagely. Charlotte and Linda also sought solace in alcohol. This led to Charlotte being arrested for various public order offences, including criminal damage as well as prostitution, while Linda had a conviction for theft and was addicted to heroin.

Linda was bringing up four children on her own. After she broke up with their father, she found herself in a relationship with a man who abused her offspring, so she returned to the family home in the Tallaght area of south Dublin, Ireland.

Mother's affair with Noor

Her parents' marriage was also at an end. Kathleen had fallen for Sheilila Said Salim, a tall, athletic African over ten years her junior.

He had arrived in Ireland in 1996, seeking asylum. Using the name Farah Swaleh Noor, he said he was a Somalian whose family had been killed in Mogadishu during the civil war. In fact, he was a Kenyan whose family were still alive. When the authorities discovered this, a deportation order was issued. He appealed and was given the right to remain, on the grounds that he had fathered a child with an Irish woman.

Noor, too, had a problem with drink. Sober, he was the perfect gentleman, but with a drink inside him he became aggressive and violent. He had dominated a former girlfriend by raping her to ensure her submission. However, her family eventually turned up to rescue her. Two other women had children by him and both accused him of rape. He had been charged with another sexual assault where a knife was found at the scene and he had also been arrested for common assault and disorder.

Despite his violent past, Kathleen – or Katie as he called her – moved him into the family home, continuing their affair under the nose of her husband. John moved out but returned home after Kathleen and Noor took a flat in 17 Richmond Cottages, a Victorian terraced house in the Summerhill district of Dublin. Their relationship became abusive, with Noor beating up Kathleen when he was drunk.

On the St Patrick's Day weekend of 2005, Linda left her children in the care of her father and joined Charlotte. They planned to meet up with their mother and Noor in the city centre. While getting ready to go out, they started drinking vodka, then took some ecstasy. Kathleen and Noor had been drinking too and started a row.

Savage killing

The row continued when the four of them got back to Richmond Cottages. In a mistaken attempt to lighten Noor's mood, Kathleen crushed a tab of ecstasy and spiked his drink. It made him amorous but the object of his desire was not Kathleen but Linda. She became flustered by his attention while Charlotte grew irritated, feeling her mother was being humiliated.

Kathleen intervened, but by then Noor had grabbed Linda around the waist and refused to let her go. Charlotte told him to take his hands off her sister and when he would not do so she went into the kitchen and got a Stanley knife. Linda was crying and Kathleen was screaming when Charlotte plunged the Stanley knife into Noor's neck. Blood spurted down his Ireland football shirt and he finally let go of Linda. She then grabbed a hammer and in a frenzy the two girls savagely attacked him. The blows continued long after he lost consciousness. His last word was 'Katie'.

Charlotte got a bread knife from the kitchen and continued stabbing him, rupturing his liver and kidneys and puncturing both

Linda (left) and Charlotte Mulhall in typical, belligerent pose.

his lungs. Linda then beat his face into a bloody pulp. The hammer blows were so savage that those that missed left deep indentations in the floorboards.

Body pieces in bin liners

They then dragged Noor's body into the bathroom. Linda later told the Gardaí that Charlotte had suggested they chop him up, but Charlotte denied it. Either way, they quickly went about the gruesome task of dismembering him with the bread knife and smashing his bones with the hammer. To steel themselves for the ordeal, they took more ecstasy.

They tried to mop up the blood with towels, but they were soon sodden. The reason for cutting him up was ostensibly to make it easier to dispose of his body but Linda also cut off Noor's penis. In one statement she made to the Gardaí, she insisted she had done this because her mother said he had raped her, though it may have been an act of revenge after he had turned his sexual attentions on her.

They cut off his lower legs with the feet still attached and then detached the thighs.

With the limbs removed, the torso was still too big to fit into plastic bin bags, so they had to cut it into two, spilling out the fetid bowels and other internal organs.

Finally, they sawed through the neck, detaching the head and leaving the body in nine separate sections.

Linda and Charlotte still needed help in disposing of the remains, so they called their father, though Kathleen was no longer speaking to him. He arrived at around 1.30 a.m. The girls sounded upset on the phone, but he assumed there had merely been a row.

'Where's Noor?' he asked.

The girls pointed to a stack of black bin liners in the corner of the room. John looked into one of them, then ran outside and threw up on the pavement. He quickly left the scene after telling them that he wanted nothing to do with any of it.

Took head to the shops

As none of the women could drive, they put the body parts into sports bags and carried them down to Ballybough Bridge, where they dumped the contents in the Royal Canal. This took several journeys. They retained the head, intending to dispose of it separately to hinder identification if the body parts were found. Meanwhile, they set about cleaning up the flat, but it was impossible to hide all the evidence of their misdeeds as Noor's blood had seeped through the carpet and soaked into the floorboards.

Later in the morning, the three women were caught on CCTV walking through the centre of Dublin. They stopped at a supermarket to buy salad rolls, which they ate as they window-shopped. One of them was carrying a suitcase, which contained Noor's head and the murder weapons. They then took the bus back to Tallaght, where they intended to bury the head in Sean Walsh Memorial Park. Charlotte tried digging a hole with the bread knife, but it was barely deep enough to cover the head, and then they threw the hammer and the knife into one of the lakes in the park.

Kathleen went home to the flat while Linda and Charlotte returned to their father's house, where they burned the suitcase they had used to transport the head. They were drunk when their sister Marie came home from work. Sobbing and distraught, Charlotte told her that Linda had killed Noor after he had tried to rape her, but Marie did not believe her.

Remains dredged up

Nothing happened for ten days, so the sisters could reasonably have thought they had got away with their grisly crime. But then swollen body parts began to surface in the canal. Passers-by assumed that someone had thrown a mannequin in. However, on 30 March someone summoned the fire brigade. They dragged some of the pieces from the water and were overwhelmed by the smell of rotting flesh. The Gardaí were then called and the area was cordoned off.

Linda and Charlotte watched the coverage on the television, exhausted from lack of sleep. At that point, Marie began to wonder whether there was any truth in what Charlotte had told her. Kathleen began to cover their tracks by calling Noor's friends, telling them that he had moved out and asking them whether they knew what had become of him.

It was not immediately obvious that the corpse was that of a black man, because the flesh was mottled and bleached. At first, the Gardaí thought they were dealing with the victim of a gangland killing, though it was not clear why the body parts had been dumped so close to one another when they could have been scattered far and wide. However, the head had not been found and the pathologist noticed that the victim's penis had been severed, leading to the theory that he had been castrated as part of a ritual killing.

Sisters tracked down

Experts on so-called 'muti' killings were contacted, but the Gardaí were quickly disabused. In muti killings the penis and other organs were harvested while the victim was still alive, giving them greater magical powers. However, there was no indication that the penis had been cut off while the victim was living. He did not seem to have been bound and there were no defence wounds on his arms and hands.

Once it was established that the victim was black, enquiries were made in the immigrant community and posters were displayed showing clothing recovered from the body. In a panic, Linda decided that she should recover Noor's head and dispose of it more securely.

She dug it up and put it in her son's school bag, intending to take it to a place she knew, out in the countryside. It was near the village of Brittas, 30 miles (48 km) south of Dublin. Fortified by a bottle of vodka, she would smash it into tiny pieces.

Noor's friend Mohammed Ali Abu Bakaar read about the body in the canal in the newspaper and recognized the Ireland football shirt in a picture accompanying the story. He contacted the Gardaí, who keyed the name Farah Swaleh Noor into their PULSE database. Noor's immigration status came up, along with his criminal record. He had been questioned over the murder of a 17-year-old girl in the Glenageary suburb of Dublin.

On file were the contact details of a woman who had borne Noor's child and had complained to the police when he had made threats. She was contacted and a DNA sample was taken from the infant's mouth, using a swab. This established that the victim was indeed Noor.

Further enquiries led the Gardaí to the flat at 17 Richmond Cottages, but Kathleen had moved out. The flat was spotless, and sections of the carpet had been removed, but it did not take long for a forensic team to find traces of blood soaked into the woodwork, establishing that this was the murder scene.

Confessions

On 3 August, Linda and Charlotte Mulhall were arrested, along with John and Kathleen. None of them were forthcoming and they were released without charge. However, John became concerned about the toll the inquiry was taking on the mental health of Linda and Charlotte and decided to confide in the police. Marie also interceded with her sisters, telling them that the police were closing in and they were going to have to face up to what they had done.

Linda eventually gave in and told the police everything she could recall. She also took them to the spot near Brittas where she said she had disposed of Noor's head, but nothing was found. Either she had forgotten the location in her drunken state or scavengers had carried off the pieces. Noor's head and penis were never recovered. Linda Mulhall was formally arrested and charged on the morning of 14 September, after her children had left for school.

When Charlotte was arrested on 17 October she insisted that Noor was already dead when she and Linda arrived at the flat. This was scarcely credible as the Gardaí already had Linda's confession. Confronted with the truth, Charlotte Mulhall broke down and confessed.

Aftermath

Unable to live with what his daughters had done, John Mulhall hanged himself in Phoenix Park shortly before Christmas. Kathleen then fled to England, where she lived under an assumed name in Birmingham and London.

At their trial, Linda and Charlotte pleaded not guilty to murder. The judge, Mr Justice Carney, dismissed Linda's excuse that she was a good mother, saying: 'If she was a good mother to four children, she would not be getting herself into a situation like that.'

Charlotte was found guilty of murder and given a mandatory life sentence, while Linda was convicted of manslaughter and sentenced to 15 years. Having sobered up in jail, Linda recalled that she had smashed up Noor's head in Phoenix Park and dumped the pieces in bins there. Presumably they are now buried deep in a landfill site.

The sisters were separated in 2008, when Charlotte was transferred out of Mountjoy Prison after someone with a mobile phone photographed her holding a knife to another prisoner's neck, apparently in jest. In the same year, their brother James Mulhall pleaded guilty to robbing two prostitutes, saying he needed the money to support his own six children along with Linda's four. He took his sister's children in after she was jailed.

After three years on the run, during which time she had got involved with another African immigrant, Kathleen returned to Ireland and pleaded guilty to impeding the investigation by helping conceal the evidence after Noor's murder. She was sentenced to five years in jail.

Linda was set free in January 2018, following a temporary release over Christmas. It was revealed that both Linda and Charlotte had been romantically involved with male prison workers.

CHAPTER 17

TAMARA SAMSONOVA

SIXTY-EIGHT-YEAR-OLD PENSIONER TAMARA Samsonova was dubbed the 'Granny Ripper' after she murdered her friend, 79-year-old Valentina Ulanova, and maybe as many as ten other people. She was caught after local dogs found a woman's limbs in the undergrowth near her block of flats in St Petersburg. While police started a major manhunt, a social worker reported Mrs Ulanova missing after Samsonova, her carer, refused them entry to her apartment. CCTV footage was checked and Samsonova was seen going in and out of her friend's flat seven times carrying body parts in bags and a saucepan thought to contain her head.

When police arrived at the flat, Samsonova admitted killing Ulanova and three other people. However, after searching the flat officers found diaries which revealed that she may have killed up to 11 victims over two decades.

Cut up alive

The murder of Valentina Ulanova resulted from a quarrel over unwashed cups. Mrs Ulanova then told Samsonova that she no longer wanted her living in the flat. Samsonova reacted by putting tranquillizers in a salad she was preparing and when Ulanova was unconscious she cut her up with a hacksaw while she was still alive. She showed the police how she had beheaded Mrs Ulanova, using a dummy.

'I came home and put the whole pack of phenazepam – 50 pills – into her Olivier salad,' Samsonova told the police. 'She liked it very much. I woke up after 2 a.m. and she was lying on the floor. So I started cutting her to pieces. It was hard for me to carry her to the bathroom, she was fat and heavy. I did everything at the kitchen where she was lying.'

The senior investigator in St Petersburg, Mikhail Timoshatov, said: 'Tamara Samsonova says that at first she made her friend sleep – and then cut her into pieces.'

Samsonova wrapped the body parts in curtains and put them into plastic bags, then dumped them near a pond in Dimitrova Street. The hips and legs were found in the garden and the head and hands were boiled in a large saucepan. These have not yet been found by the police and nor have the internal organs. It was thought that they were thrown into the rubbish skip, which was collected the following Saturday, though Samsonova may have eaten them. She refused to tell the police where the head was.

CCTV images showed a figure in a blue raincoat dragging bags that left a trail of blood. It took Samsonova two hours to dispose of the body on the night of the murder.

Samsonova told the police that Ulanova had told her: 'I am tired of you.' She then asked her to leave and go back and live in her own apartment.

'I was scared to live at home,' Samsonova said. 'I panicked.' By killing Ulanova, she said she could 'live here in peace for another five months, until her relatives turn up, or somebody else'.

Grisly diary entries

Mrs Ulanova was not her first victim. The torso of a man – minus his arms, legs and head – had been found in the same street 12 years earlier. His business card, which was found in her flat, and a diary entry describing his tattoo linked Samsonova to the murder.

The diaries were found among her collection of books on black magic and astrology. They were written in Russian, German and English. Before retiring, Samsonova had worked in a hotel and was proficient in foreign languages. The police regarded the diary as a puzzle they had to decipher, matching entries to bodies found around

Tamara Samsonova, dubbed the 'Granny Ripper', may have killed up to 11 victims over two decades.

the city. However, some entries were more straightforward and included accounts of the murders of former lodgers.

'I killed my tenant Volodya, cut him to pieces in the bathroom with a knife, put the pieces of his body in plastic bags and threw them away in the different parts of Frunzensky district,' she wrote.

Another victim, Sergei Potynavin, a 44-year-old native of Norilsk, was killed after an argument on 6 September 2003. Again she dismembered the body, taking the body parts out of the flat in plastic bags and dumping them. Traces of his blood were found in her bathroom.

Such blood-curdling confessions were found among everyday entries which said that she slept badly, skipped a meal or took her medicine. One read: 'I woke at 5 a.m. I am drinking coffee. Then I do work around the house.' It went on to say that she went out to buy marshmallows. Another entry made it clear that she liked living with Valentina Ulanova, whom she addressed by the diminutive Valya, even saying: 'I love Valya.'

The diaries also included poems, songs and her reflections on life. Other entries indicated that she ate some of her victims. The police said she had a particular penchant for gouging out their lungs and consuming them. Samsonova also admitted to 11 murders, without giving details. During her murderous career, Samsonova was admitted to psychiatric hospitals three times and it was thought she was suffering from schizophrenia.

Missing family members

It was feared that she had also disposed of her husband, whom she reported missing in 2005. She told the police that he had met another woman. However, he has yet to be found, dead or alive.

At the time he disappeared, neighbour Marina Krivenko recalled: 'We had some coffee in her kitchen, and we chatted. She already looked strange then. She told me about her husband, that he left home and did not come back. And at that moment I noticed some kind of pleasure in Tamara's eyes.'

Samsonova's mother-in-law also disappeared and she admitted to an old school friend, 67-year-old Anna Batalina, that she was suspected of killing her.

Mrs Batalina was also thought to have been in danger after Samsonova flew into a rage with her, screaming: 'I'll kill you. I'll cut you to pieces. I will throw the pieces out for the dogs. Don't make me angry.'

Interest in Chikatilo

Mrs Krivenko had known Samsonova for 15 years and said she was very interested in the bloodthirsty killer Andrei Chikatilo. Known as the Rostov Ripper or the Butcher of Rostov, Chikatilo sexually assaulted, murdered and mutilated at least 53 women and children between 1978 and 1990. He was executed with a bullet in the back of the head in 1994.

'She gathered information about him and how he committed his murders,' the neighbour said.

Other Russian killers have compared themselves to Chikatilo. The 'Chessboard Maniac' Alexander Pichushkin set out to beat Chikatilo's death toll by killing one person for every square on the chessboard. He nearly made it. In 2007, he was jailed for life for killing 62 people, largely in Bitsa Park in Moscow.

The following year, 62-year-old ex-detective and serial killer Serhiy Tkach boasted: 'I'm not a man, I'm a beast. Same as Chikatilo.' Convicted of 29 murders and 11 attempted murders, he claimed to have killed more than 200 people over 25 years.

Another former cop, Mikhail Popkov, also proudly compared himself to Chikatilo, according to the local prosecutor. In 2015, he was convicted of 22 murders. but was under investigation for at least another 30.

Alexander Bychkov was also a Chikatilo follower, as well as being a cannibal. His mother saw him paste newspaper cuttings about Chikatilo into a scrapbook.

By the age of 23, in 2012, he had killed 11 elderly men and eaten them. He had the same signature as Chikatilo – that is, he stabbed his victims in the eyes.

Eccentric behaviour

For years Samsonova had boasted to friends that, one day: 'I will be popular and famous.' She told them she would eventually cause a 'sensation', without explaining how or why.

Mrs Krivenko reported other instances of eccentric behaviour.

'I came to live here with my husband,' she said. 'I used to go to Tamara's flat and call from her phone. She looked a lot better 15 years ago, and her flat too was a lot more attractive than now. She looked after her appearance, and had this weird habit of sitting topless with her back to the window, making sure that her silhouette was seen by the neighbours.'

Apparently, Mr Krivenko found her naked body appealing. Mrs Krivenko also said that Samsonova boasted about her excellent German and English, and admitted lending her a hacksaw some years earlier, which she never returned.

Glad to be caught

Despite facing the death penalty, Samsonova was more concerned about the publicity her arrest had attracted. She told reporters: 'I knew you would come. It's such a disgrace for me; all the city will know.'

However, she bore no hostility towards the journalists, blowing a kiss to them. She also refused to take the charges seriously. When the judge, Roman Chebotaryov, asked her to address the court, she said: 'It's stuffy in here, can I go out?'

She seemed relieved at having been caught, telling the judge: 'I was getting ready for this court action for dozens of years. It was all done deliberately . . . There is no way to live. With this last murder, I closed the chapter.'

The judge said: 'I am asked to detain you. What do you think?'

'You decide, your honour,' she replied. 'After all, I am guilty and I deserve punishment.'

Detained for life

When she was told that she would remain in custody, she beamed and clapped her hands.

While admitting to murdering Mrs Ulanova and others, Samsonova refused to co-operate with the police over other suspected killings. Although the police did not rule out further charges, without finding the body parts prosecution would be problematic.

'We may never know the extent of this granny's killings,' one source close to the investigation said. 'She's either much more stupid, or much smarter, than she seems.'

After the hearing, Samsonova was put on a high-security train and taken under guard to a psychiatric prison hospital in Kazan, the capital of Tatarstan, nearly 1,000 miles (1,609 km) away, for assessment. This was where Joseph Stalin's secret police used to lock up political prisoners. It is now called the Kazan Psychiatric Hospital of Special Purpose with Intensive Guarding.

In 2017, Judge Pavel Smirnov decreed that she should spend the rest of her life in a mental institution, after a diagnosis of paranoid schizophrenia. The court heard that she still represented a threat to those around her, as well as herself, and that she required 'intensive monitoring'.

CHAPTER 18

JUANA BARRAZA

THE POLICE IN Mexico City made a fundamental mistake when hunting for *El Mataviejitas* ('The Old Lady Killer') – the serial killer who was murdering women over 60, strangling them with her bare hands or with cables, scarves and stockings. They assumed that the masculine figure seen leaving crime scenes dressed in women's clothing was a transvestite. In fact, she was a female professional wrestler known in the ring as *La Dama del Silencio*.

Early life

The real name of wrestling's 'Lady of Silence' was Juana Dayanara Barraza Samperio. She was born in 1956 in rural Hidalgo, Mexico, just north of Mexico City, to an alcoholic prostitute who left the child's father, a policeman, soon after she was born. The parent–child relationship was troubled. A silent child, Juana barely spoke as an infant. Being withdrawn hampered her at school and she never learned to read or write anything beyond her name.

When she was 11, her mother sold her to a man in exchange for three beers. He sexually abused her and she suffered miscarriages at the ages of 13 and 16, as well as giving birth to the first of her four children. After her mother died of cirrhosis of the liver, Juana left for Mexico City. There she had another three children from a series of failed marriages. Her eldest son died at the age of 24 after being beaten with a baseball bat by muggers.

Juana Barraza seems to have blamed her many misfortunes on her mother and criminologists believe this was the motivation for her murder spree.

Wrestling career

During the 1980s and 1990s, Barraza toured Mexico while taking part in a form of wrestling known as *lucha libre*, or free fighting. The fighters wore masks and had cartoon-character names. They were identified as either *técnicos* – good guys who fought by the rules – or *rudos* – villains who broke them. Interviewed by a TV channel while attending a wrestling match a few weeks before her arrest, Barraza described herself as '*rudo* to the core'.

She was often seen in the front rows at the established arenas, selling popcorn. Organizing wrestling events for small-town fiestas, she occasionally took to fighting in the ring herself. She later told the police that she had picked the professional name *La Dama del Silencio* 'because I am quiet and keep myself to myself'.

Fairly low down in the rankings, she was getting just 300 to 500 pesos a fight – between £15 and £25 ($20-$33) – and began shoplifting and housebreaking to support her children. In 1996, she and a friend began stealing from elderly people. They dressed up as nurses to gain access to their homes and stole whatever they could when they got inside. However, her friend's lover was a corrupt cop who demanded a 12,000-peso (£480/$640) bribe from Barraza in return for not arresting her.

When Barraza retired from the ring in the year 2000, her financial situation grew worse. At the same time, a spate of brutal murders of

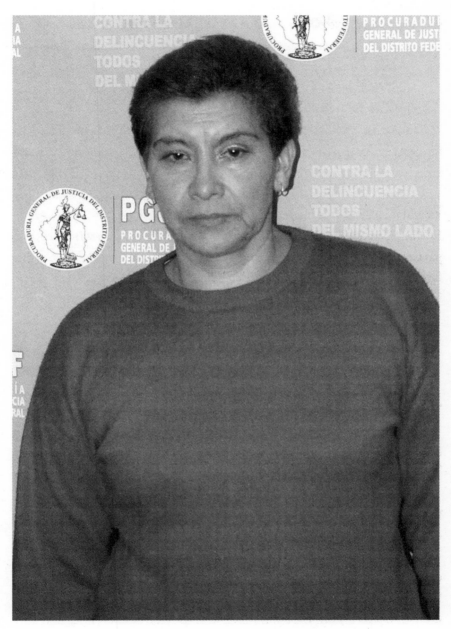

Juana Barraza – when she was 11, her mother sold her to a man in exchange for three beers.

elderly women began in Mexico City. The press dubbed the killer *El Mataviejitas*, assuming the perpetrator was a male – the female version is *La Mataviejitas*.

Thought to be a man

The first murder associated with Barraza was that of María de la Luz González Anaya on 25 November 2002. Once Barraza had gained entrance to her apartment, González made comments that Barraza considered derogatory. Infuriated, she beat González before strangling her to death with her bare hands. Three months later, she killed again.

After a year, the police had enough evidence and witness statements to conclude that a serial killer was at work. The killer, they said, was a tall person with rough features who was posing as a city council nurse or a social worker to gain the victims' trust. In December 2003, the police released a wanted poster with two eyewitness sketches of the *Mataviejitas* – one slightly feminine and another more masculine.

Mexico City police had an eyewitness account that described the killer as 'a man, dressed as a woman, or a robust woman, dressed in white, height between 1.70 and 1.75 metres [5ft 7in–5ft 9in], robust complexion, light brown, oval face, wide cheeks, blond hair, delineated eyebrows, [and] approximately 45 years old'.

The Mexican Department of Justice also developed a psychological profile after examining cases of serial killers who targeted elderly women in France and Spain. This specified that the killer was 'a man with homosexual preferences, victim of childhood physical abuse, [who] lived surrounded by women, he could have had a grandmother or lived with an elderly person, has resentment to that feminine figure, and possesses great intelligence'. Consequently, the police announced that they were looking for a homosexual man, who was 'transvestite or transgendered'. They then arrested 49 transvestite prostitutes, who were all released when their fingerprints didn't match those at the crime scenes. Another red herring was the fact that at least three of the victims owned a print of an 18th-century painting by French artist Jean-Baptiste Greuze, *Boy in a Red Waistcoat*.

The police then came to believe that the killer was dead and checked the fingerprints of bodies in the morgue.

Operation Parks and Gardens

Meanwhile, Barraza continued approaching her victims on the street or knocking on their doors, pretending to be a city council nurse or a social worker. At first she had simply worn white clothes, but she later acquired a nurse's uniform. She would gain their trust by offering them a massage or help in obtaining medicines and benefits. If her victims were distracted, she strangled them directly. If not, she would beat them, using moves she had learned in her wrestling career. Though she carried a bag with medical equipment, she usually strangled her victims manually or with a ligature taken from the victim's own home, which she would leave at the crime scene. Then she would rob them.

The killing of 82-year-old Carmen Camila González Miguel on 28 September 2005 – mother of prominent Mexican criminologist Luis Rafael Moreno González – spurred the police into launching a special operation under the name of *Operación Parques y Jardines* – 'Operation Parks and Gardens'. Patrols in the areas where the killer was active increased and pamphlets were distributed advising old ladies to be wary of strangers. It was reported that the police even paid elderly women to act as bait in park areas they were keeping under surveillance.

Caught in the act

On 25 January 2006, Barraza entered the house of Ana María de los Reyes Alfaro in the Venustiano Carranza area of the capital by the simple device of asking for a glass of water. Once inside, she picked up a stethoscope that happened to be lying on the living room table and used it to strangle her elderly hostess. She was seen by a tenant as she left the apartment, shortly before he stumbled over the corpse of his landlady. He raised the alarm and she was arrested by a passing police patrol, who said she also confessed to three other killings.

Ismael Alvarado Ruiz, one of two policemen who made the arrest, said: 'My partner and I caught her by the arms and took her back to the patrol car. We went back to the house, and everything was scattered all around.'

Barraza was found in possession of a social worker's identification card and pension forms. She used them to gain entry to victims' homes by posing as a government employee who could sign them up to welfare programmes. A search of her home revealed a trophy room complete with newspaper clippings of the murders and mementoes, such as ornaments or religious items, taken from the victims. There was also an altar to Jesús Malverde and Santa Muerte (Saint Death), two folk saints often honoured by Mexican criminals.

Media circus

Her arrest was a media circus when she was paraded before the cameras. It is common practice in Mexico to let reporters interview suspects at the crime scene.

'Yes, I did it,' Barraza said, smiling for the television cameras. 'Just because I'm going to pay for it, that doesn't mean they're going to hang all the crimes on me.'

She also denied pretending to be a social worker.

'That's a lie. I wasn't carrying the documents they have there,' she said, maintaining that when she went to the victims' homes she offered to help with laundry or other household chores. But she offered no clues to her motive.

'You'll know why I did it when you read my statement to the police,' she said.

She was then posed beside a bust of the prime suspect, made during the hunt. With her cropped hair and distinctive mole, she bore a striking resemblance to the model. The police also released photographs of Barraza recreating the murder of Reyes for detectives, along with videoed excerpts of her police interrogation. All this was done before she had even been formally remanded in custody.

Barraza's fingerprints matched those found at ten murder scenes, along with one attempted murder. In the end, she was charged with 30 murders – though it was thought she had committed many more.

'I only killed one little old lady. Not the others,' Barraza told the court. 'It isn't right to pin the others on me.' Asked about her motive, she said simply: 'I got angry.'

Attempts to have her found not guilty by reason of insanity failed. She was pronounced guilty of 11 murders, plus 12 robberies. In each case, she was tied to the crime scene by fingerprint evidence. Although she was sentenced to 759 years in prison, under Mexican law she can only serve 50 years and will be due for parole in 2058, when she will be 102.

When she heard the sentence, she said: 'Let God forgive me and do not abandon me.'

CHAPTER 19

ENRIQUETA MARTÍ

KNOWN AS THE Vampire of Barcelona, Enriqueta Martí worked as a prostitute before branching out into kidnapping children for wealthy paedophiles. She also killed street children to make costly beauty products and love potions for her upper-class and callous clientele.

Works as prostitute

In 1888, 20-year-old Enriqueta Martí arrived at the railway station in Barcelona from Sant Feliu de Llobregat in Catalonia. The city was booming at the time. Industrialization had brought a flood of peasants into Barcelona from the surrounding countryside and the merchant class grew wealthy on the backs of the poor. First of all, Martí worked as a domestic servant for a wealthy family who lived in the upmarket l'Eixample area of the city. A lowly drudge, she quickly came to envy the lavish lifestyle of her employers.

Barcelona was holding a World's Fair that year and the luxury displayed there was in stark contrast to the grinding poverty of the slum districts such as El Raval, then known as the Barrio Chino, but Enriqueta soon learned that the rich would pay handsomely for anything they wanted, including sex.

An attractive young woman, Enriqueta sought to better herself materially by quitting her domestic job and going to work as a prostitute in a high-class brothel. Among her numerous clients were men of wealth and position.

In 1895, Enriqueta married the painter Juan Pujaló but the marriage failed as Enriqueta could not resist continuing to see her wealthy clients. The couple broke up five or six times before splitting for good in 1907.

Kidnaps children

The economy of the port suffered a downturn with the Spanish–American War of 1898, during which Spain lost its remaining colonies in the Americas and the Pacific. But money was always there to be had. In the early 1900s, Martí rented a small apartment in Barrio

Chino, where she ran a brothel. Knowing the tastes of some wealthy men, she also started kidnapping children and forcing them into prostitution. During the day, she would dress in rags and join bread queues, looking for abandoned waifs whom she would clean up for her clients. It was a lucrative trade and at night she was able to don expensive clothing and jewellery and mingle with high society in the Casino de la Arrabassada and the El Liceu opera house. This brought her into contact with wealthy women. To expand her business, she began selling them herbal remedies and beauty products, which were made up in another of the apartments she rented.

Enriqueta Martí married a painter but the marriage failed because she could not resist seeing her clients from a high-class brothel.

In 1909 the conscription of reservists to fight in the unpopular war against the Berbers in Morocco provoked a general strike and rioting and the government in Madrid sent in troops. Over 100 civilians were killed in what became known as *La semana trágica* – 'Tragic Week'. Martial law was declared, thousands were detained and Martí's brothel was raided. Although she was taken into custody for procuring children as young as three for sex, a young client from a wealthy family was also arrested in the raid. Consequently, the paperwork was lost and the case never came to trial.

Blood cure

Martí must have believed she was now above the law. At the time, people believed that drinking blood was a cure for the tuberculosis that was then ravaging the city. Upper-class women also thought that children's blood preserved the bloom of youth and their fat would prevent the skin from ageing. Martí provided both of these items. She also pounded bones into powder to make her expensive preparations.

Rumours began to circulate that young children were going missing, but the authorities did nothing. In fact, the civil governor of Barcelona, Manuel Portela Valladares, even issued a statement in 1911 denying it was happening. The last thing he wanted was a further intervention by the government in Madrid.

Then on 10 February 1912, a young girl named Teresita Guitart Congost disappeared. This time there was an outcry against the authorities, who again seemed to be doing nothing about a missing child. However, Claudia Elías, a neighbour of Martí's, saw a girl answering Teresita's description peering out of her window at 29 Ponent Street. She knew Martí had no children, so she confided her suspicions to other neighbours and word soon reached the ears of the police.

Young girls found

When the police raided the flat on 27 February, they found two young girls. Martí claimed that she had found Teresita the previous day, when she was wandering the streets lost and hungry. But Claudia Elías had seen the girl five days earlier. Martí then claimed that the other child, Angelita, was her own.

The two girls were questioned. Teresita said she had been lured by the promise of sweets. When she realized she was being taken far from home she asked to be taken back, but Martí covered her head and took her on to number 29. She told the police that when Martí got her back to the flat she cut her hair short and told her that she no longer had any parents. Martí was to be her stepmother and her name was no longer Teresita but Felicidad. After that she was maltreated and fed only stale bread and potatoes.

Teresita went on to say that she and Angelita had often been left on their own in the apartment. They were told not to go near the windows or out on to the balcony. There was also a room in which they found a bag containing bloodstained clothes and a boning knife also covered with blood.

Murders small boy

Angelita added that before Teresita arrived there had been a five-year-old boy called Pepito living there, but one day she had seen 'mama' stab him to death.

'Mama did not realize that I saw her take Pepito, put him on the dining table and kill him,' she said. After seeing this she ran back to her bed and pretended to sleep.

Martí claimed that Angelita was her daughter by her husband Juan Pujaló, but hearing of Martí's arrest Pujaló went to the police and told them that he and his wife had no children. It was later discovered that Martí had stolen Angelita at birth from his sister

Maria. She had been assisting at the delivery and had convinced Maria that her baby was stillborn.

Asked about Pepito, Martí said that she had been looking after him for a family who could no longer care for him, though she could not name the family or provide any other identification. When she was asked where he was, she said he had gone to the countryside because he was ill.

Pepito's identity was soon revealed. After Martí was arrested, the national newspapers carried daily stories about the case under the headline 'The Mysteries of Barcelona'. In response, a peasant woman from Alcañiz made contact, saying she had arrived in Barcelona with a baby boy in her arms six years earlier, aiming to find work. Faint from hunger, she sat down on the doorstep of a house and a woman approached her.

'What a pretty babe, do you want me to give her a little breast?' the woman asked.

The peasant woman said the child no longer suckled, so the stranger then offered to get her a glass of milk. On the way to the dairy, she volunteered to carry the child.

While the peasant woman was drinking the milk, the stranger offered to get her some bread. She left, taking the baby, and did not come back. Six years later, the woman from Alcañiz identified the woman who had taken her baby as Enriqueta Martí. Sadly, it was clear that her child was now dead, killed just days before Martí was arrested.

Body parts discovered

The apartment was searched and the bag containing the clothing and the knife was found, along with another bag which held the bones of children. Other children's clothing was also discovered. In another room, the police found pitchers and a washbasin containing the raw materials – blood, fat, bones and hair – for the preparations Martí sold, along with jars containing the finished products, ready for sale.

Asked to explain the presence of the body parts, first Martí said she was studying human anatomy and then she insisted that she was a healer who was merely servicing a wealthy clientele.

Three other flats rented by Martí under another name were raided and more jars were found. False walls and ceilings also hid human body parts. The remains of more children, some as young as three, were found buried in the garden at one of the properties and the police also seized a book of recipes compiled by Martí, along with a list of her clients.

Mystery death

Martí admitted procuring children for paedophiles, but it was her clients who were monsters, not her, she said. The women who bought her tonics and creams knew what they were made from, but they were unconcerned because they thought street children were no better than trash. Martí insisted that she was simply a businesswoman supplying a demand.

There was intense interest in the names of Martí's clientele, but these were not released and the date of her trial kept being put back. She tried to commit suicide but the authorities told the press that she was being watched by three prisoner-trustees who shared her cell.

Eventually it was announced that Enriqueta Martí had died in the Reina Amàlia jail on 12 May 1913, after a long illness. However, many believed that she had been hanged in the prison yard by her fellow prisoners, who had been paid by her wealthy clients to ensure she would never come to trial and spill the beans.

CHAPTER 20

LOUISE GARDNER

ON 14 MARCH 2008, a girl on a pink mountain bike cycled up Whitfield Road in the Anfield district of Liverpool, pursued by a black Fiat Punto. It pulled to a halt and a woman with long blonde hair got out and shouted to a gaggle of teenagers on the street: 'Girls, grab her for me!'

The girl on the bicycle quickly rode off, turning into Woodville Terrace, a cul-de-sac. But the blond woman chased after her, shouting: 'I am going to kill you.' She was followed by the teenagers, eager to witness the outcome.

Trapped there, the cyclist was pushed off her bike. She was screaming 'Get off, get off!' while she was being kicked, stamped on and punched. Her attacker then pulled a knife, stabbed her in the chest and head and slashed her face. Then she walked away, got back into her car and drove off.

One witness, a boy of 15, later told the police that the victim tried to raise her head, but couldn't. Local resident Elizabeth Blanchard, a grandmother, was watching television with her husband Brian when her daughter Carla suddenly ran in shouting: 'There's a girl, I think she's dead.'

Carla was clearly distressed.

'I could see the panic in her face,' said Mrs Blanchard. 'I went out and I could hear people shouting: "She's dead, she's dead!"'

Mrs Blanchard pushed her way through the crowd to find the victim sprawled on the ground.

'She didn't appear to be breathing so I shook her chin gently and I pinched her ear, but I got no response,' she said. 'I checked her airways and turned her on to her right hand side and checked her pulse and I couldn't find a pulse.'

Someone called 999 and Mrs Blanchard followed telephone instructions on how to administer CPR and mouth-to-mouth resuscitation, but it did no good.

'I said to the operator: "I think she's dead,"' said Mrs Blanchard.

The police arrived within minutes and Detective Sergeant Mark Baker, a veteran police officer, said he was shocked by the level of violence the victim had suffered. It was one of the most horrific incidents he had witnessed.

Dead on arrival

When the ambulance arrived, the girl was taken to the Royal Liverpool Hospital, where she was pronounced dead on arrival. At the crime scene, the police set about interviewing witnesses and searching for the murder weapon.

It was soon discovered that while the victim looked like a teenage girl she was in fact a 26-year-old mother of two. When the police discovered where she lived, they broke in to find an infant who had been left alone for 24 hours.

Fortunately, the child was in good health and had suffered no ill effects. She was taken into care.

The victim's name was Rachel Jones. She was from Chester and had moved to Liverpool seven years earlier, after having a baby. The police soon discovered who the perpetrator was too. Witnesses said she had shouted out something about a broken window and the local police station had a complaint on record about a similar incident. It had been made by 25-year-old Louise Gardner, who lived with her mother Diane, less than a mile from Woodville Terrace. Louise was taken into custody awaiting a hearing at the local magistrates' court the following morning, where she was charged with murder.

Family feud

It soon became apparent that there was more at issue than a broken window. Rachel's twin sister Becky told the police that a feud had been brewing between Rachel and the Gardner family for some years. Soon after Rachel moved to Liverpool from Chester at the age of 19, she got to know Louise Gardner's sister Vicky. She was a party girl who took Rachel's mind off the full-time responsibility of looking after newborn Demi-Lee with little help from the father.

However, the party scene quickly grew too heavy for Rachel. Vicky's friends would turn up at Rachel's flat with drink and drugs for an impromptu rave and then others would flock to the venue. This was not the ideal situation in which to bring up a young daughter.

Rachel moved house, but the partygoers soon tracked her down. When she was away visiting her mother, some of the party people kicked in the door of her flat and held a party, leaving her home devastated.

'They had gone around to sit in the house and have a party, but because Rachel was not there, they had kicked the door in to have a party and then wrecked the place,' said Becky. 'Our Rachel could never understand why she did it to her. It all started over that.'

Louise Gardner – when she met Rachel Jones in the street, it was only the presence of their children that prevented the confrontation from descending into violence.

Rachel blamed Vicky. The first confrontation occurred a few months later, when Rachel spotted Vicky when she was out shopping in the BHS department store. Rachel would not accept Vicky's apology; they argued and blows were exchanged. The disagreement then became a family feud. Louise Gardner took her younger sister Vicky's side, while Becky urged Rachel to concentrate on looking after Demi-Lee rather than fuelling the fight with the Gardners, who were rumoured to be associated with the local crime family.

The feud might have died a natural death if Louise had not chosen to taunt Rachel every time she saw her in the area. Meanwhile, there was a brief reconciliation between Rachel and Demi-Lee's father, resulting in a second baby but no further advancement in the relationship. Rachel then had another daughter, Atalia, to look after.

But the feud between Rachel and Louise did not die down. When they met in the street, the only thing that stopped the confrontation descending into violence was the presence of their children. Rachel was usually pushing a pram, while Louise was a mother of two as well.

However, someone threw paint-stripper over the Gardners' car and then paint was hurled at the house Louise shared with her mother. Louise became convinced that Rachel was responsible – indeed, Becky confirmed that she was.

'She thought Vicky was her friend and she could not let it go,' said Becky. 'I kept saying to her: "Let it go, it's gone now, you have had a fight."'

The feud simmered on and then came an act of vandalism that Louise was certain Rachel had committed.

Brick through the window

'She happened to ring me up, mentioning it,' said Rachel's lover, David Edge. 'She brought it up and she happened to say something like: "I don't care if they stab me." I don't think she really expected it to happen.'

On the evening of 14 March 2008, Rachel cycled to the Gardners' house in Mallow Road and threw a brick through the window. She did not seek to hide what she had done, but pulled back her hood and laughed. Louise Gardner reported the incident to the police, but she did not tell them that Rachel Jones had thrown the brick, even though she had been clearly identified. What possessed Rachel to do this no one knows. Demi-Lee was staying elsewhere that night, but it was out of character for Rachel, a devoted mother, to leave Atalia on her own.

Although only a window had been broken, someone could easily have been injured, if only by flying glass. Clearly the feud had to stop. Louise Gardner picked up a knife, got in the family car and hunted Rachel down. That was not difficult because she knew where Rachel lived and what route she would be taking home. During the pursuit her emotions did not calm and by the time Louise abandoned the car and pursed Rachel on foot her blood was high.

Chilling injuries

'I just switched,' she said. 'I was just knackered running and I could not breathe, and then I have done that with a knife and got all the energy. I could not stop it. I can just remember stabbing her in the chest and then in her face. I took hold of her hair and then I slashed her face. I knew where I had stabbed her with the knife, but I could not control what I was doing. Nothing was stopping me. It was like my body did not want to stop.'

The accounts of witnesses were chilling. First Louise stabbed Rachel in the back of the skull and then she dragged her from the bike by her hair and stamped on her head. In all, Rachel was stabbed 14 times. Twice the blade penetrated her head. A slash across the face was so forceful that it broke Rachel's jaw. If she had survived, she would have been disfigured for life.

At first the police had difficulty identifying the victim, saying only that she was aged between 16 and 20 and about 5ft 6in (1.68 m) tall, with dark brown, shoulder-length hair. Eventually, Rachel was identified from her tattoos. There was a garland of flowers around her navel and she had the name 'Atalia' on her right hip and 'Demi-Lee' on her right foot, with a rose entwined in the letters.

Arrested and charged

When Louise was arrested and charged with murder 14 hours later, she claimed that Rachel had provoked her and that it was she who had brought the knife along. It had then somehow fallen into Louise's hands and she had used it in self-defence. However, the murder weapon was a distinctive CrossCut lock knife, which was notoriously difficult to open and close. Its box was found behind the microwave oven in the Gardners' house.

When Louise was asked what she had done with the knife after the murder, she said it had been thrown down a drain. When it was recovered, the knife was found to be closed, showing that Louise knew how it operated.

Gardner also said that she had dumped her bloody clothes in a wheelie bin, but in fact she had left them with a friend. About an hour after the attack, she had turned up at the home of Elizabeth Kerwin and given her the clothes in a plastic bag, saying she had been in a fight but did not know what had become of her opponent – though if she had died she would hand herself in. The clothes were found in the cupboard under Kerwin's stairs.

Rachel's twin sister Becky found the turn of events hard to take in.

'My sister was a quiet girl, but she had lots of friends. She didn't go into town much or go out drinking,' she said. 'I've gone back to the scene where she was killed – it was really hard. I can't get my head round why this all happened. The last few days don't feel real, I keep thinking that Rachel is about to come home and pick up the baby.'

Life sentence

Although Gardner admitted the slaying, she pleaded not guilty to murder, on the grounds that she was provoked. On 8 September 2008, a jury failed to reach a verdict in the case, but at a retrial the following February Louise Gardner was convicted. Rachel's friends and family cheered and hugged each other when they heard the verdict. Becky said: 'It's been a long time coming.'

Gardner was given a mandatory life sentence with a minimum tariff of 16 years.

'You have shown not one particle of remorse,' said Judge Gerald Clifton when sentencing. 'You ended the life of a young mother and deprived two very young children of their mother.'

Gardner was unfazed. She smiled and waved to her family as she was taken down, even though her own children would be left without a mother as they grew up.

'This was an extremely brutal and sustained attack which resulted in Rachel suffering horrific injuries which led to her death,' said Detective Chief Inspector Richie Davies of the Merseyside Police. 'Louise Gardner carried out this brutal attack on a residential street in front of a group of young people, some of whom have had to have counselling. This terrible attack and the injuries they witnessed will live with them for a long time.'

Becky added a tribute to her sister, saying:

She was such a pretty girl. I can't believe anyone could do this to my sister. She's been killed so young; she hasn't lived her life. We had to watch our dad die when we were 16. Rachel has had a hard life. She did not deserve this. . . . She loved her children to bits. She was a mum, that's what she did and what she lived for. As twin sisters, me and Rachel were really close. I cannot bear it. Atalia thinks that I'm her mum. We've had to tell Demi-Lee that she fell off her bike and her mum is not coming back.

CHAPTER 21

PHOOLAN DEVI

AT THE AGE of just 17, Phoolan Devi committed the largest bandit massacre in India since independence. What made it all the more notable in the eyes of the nation was that a low-caste woman had murdered 22 men of a vastly higher caste. After 11 years in jail she went on to become a member of parliament, though she could neither read nor write. She also achieved worldwide fame thanks to the Oscar-nominated Bollywood biopic *Bandit Queen* which, according to *The Washington Post*, portrayed her as a 'modern-day Indian Robin Hood and Bonnie Parker, with a touch of Gloria Steinem'.

Early years

Born in 1963 in a remote village in Uttar Pradesh in northern India, Phoolan Devi was of the lowly Mallah caste of boatmen or fishermen. Her family were poor because her parents had four daughters before they produced a son and this allowed a male cousin named Maiyadin to cheat her father out of 15 acres of land that he owned. At the age of ten, Phoolan started a battle to reclaim the land. She taunted her cousin in the village square, calling him all manner of things in front of his high-caste friends. Then with her 12-year-old sister she staged a sit-in on Maiyadin's land until he knocked her unconscious with a brick.

When she was 11, her parents married her off to a man three times her age from a distant village, in exchange for a cow. This was not unusual in rural India and she conceded that her parents did this with the best of intentions. Her husband was a widower who had money and they thought she would have a better life.

'No one knew that he was not a man, he was a monster,' she said.

Despite her young age, he forced himself on her sexually and beat her frequently. She ran away at the age of 12, walking over 700 miles (1,125 km) home. In Indian society this was a disgrace and her mother advised her to commit suicide by jumping into the village well. Instead, she married a cousin who was already married. This gave her a reputation for promiscuity. She was scorned by the men of the land-owning Thakur caste and was said to bathe naked in the sacred Yamuna river.

Meanwhile, she continued her battle with Maiyadin, arguing her father's case before the Allahabad High Court. Her cousin countered this by accusing her of stealing from his house. She was then arrested and spent a month in jail, where she was beaten and raped by the police. At a later date, she said she was left 'a whimpering piece of rubbish in the corner of a dirty room with rats staring me in the eye'.

Becomes bandit

She was then seized by a gang of bandits, or dacoits, who camped outside the village. Their leader, the notoriously cruel Babu Gujjar, brutalized her for three days. Babu Gujjar was upper-caste, but his deputy, Vikram Mallah, was a member of Phoolan's Mallah caste, so he took pity on her and shot Babu Gujjar dead. Phoolan then became

Former 'Bandit Queen' turned politician, Phoolan Devi champions the rights of women at Adalhat, India, 15 April 1996.

Vikram's mistress. Together they held up trains, ransacked and looted upper-caste villages and murdered and kidnapped, ostensibly in the name of justice in a caste war. As well as introducing Phoolan into the ways of the dacoits, Vikram had her long hair cropped and taught her how to fire a gun, after which she became a crack shot. He also bought her a transistor radio and a cassette player, so she could listen to the music from the films she loved.

They hid out in bandit country – the ravines and jungles of Uttar and Madhya Pradesh – and women composed songs about the exploits of the low-caste village girl who became a dacoit and was vindicated, her honour restored. According to one popular ballad sung in the village, Vikram taught her one key lesson: 'If you are going to kill, kill 20, not just one. For if you kill 20, your fame will spread; if you kill only one, they will hang you as a murderess.'

Phoolan revelled in the myth and had a rubber stamp made, which she used as a letterhead. It read: 'Phoolan Devi, dacoit beauty; beloved of Vikram Mallah, Emperor of Dacoits.'

Before each of their criminal exploits, Phoolan insisted that they worship at one of the many temples of Durga, the weapon-wielding Hindu goddess who is depicted riding a tiger. She also read omens. One night, while they were sitting around a camp fire, she felt a snake slithering up her thigh. She flung it aside and then insisted that the band pick up their guns and flee. Ten minutes after they left, the police descended on their campsite.

'God sends his own signals,' Phoolan said.

Behmai massacre

In August 1980 she saw a crow sitting in a dead tree near their jungle camp and begged Vikram to move on, but this time he refused. That night he was shot dead by Sri and Lala Ram Singh, two upper-caste bandits seeking revenge for the murder of Babu Gujjar.

The Ram brothers bound Phoolan and took her to the village of Behmai, where she was kept in a filthy hut and gang-raped by Thakur men until she passed out. After three weeks, she was let out and forced to walk the length of the village naked to collect water while the Thakur men looked on, laughing and spitting at her.

Eventually, Phoolan was rescued by a priest from a nearby village and went on to form her own gang. Seventeen months later, on St Valentine's Day, Phoolan and her followers returned to Behmai in police uniforms. The villagers were surprised to notice that the party was led by a young girl wearing bright lipstick, with her nails painted red and her hair cut in an unusual bob. She carried a Sten gun and wore a bandolier of ammunition across her chest.

Once the village was sealed off by her men, she mounted the parapet of the village well and raised a megaphone to her lips.

'Listen to me. If you love your lives, hand over all of the cash, silver, and gold you have,' she said. 'And listen again! I know that Lala Ram Singh and Sri Ram Singh are hiding in this village. If you don't hand them over to me, I will stick my gun into your butts and tear them apart. This is Phoolan Devi speaking. *Jai Durga Mata!*' – 'Victory to Durga the Mother Goddess!'

The village was looted, but Phoolan's men could not find the Ram brothers and the villagers denied ever seeing the two men.

'You are lying!' Phoolan yelled. 'I will teach you to tell the truth!'

She had all of the young men rounded up and then spat on them.

'Unless you tell me where those bastards are, I will roast you alive,' she said.

When they continued to say they had never seen the two brothers, she tore off their turbans and hit them in the groin with the butt of her gun. Then she had them marched out to the river, where they were forced to kneel. In a burst of gunfire 30 men fell and 22 of them were killed.

The St Valentine's Day Massacre of the Thakur men made Phoolan a folk hero among lower-caste Indians, who called her the Bandit Queen, the Goddess of the Flowers and the Beautiful Bandit. Upper-caste men still looked down on her, saying: 'For every man this girl has killed, she has slept with two. Sometimes she sleeps with them first, before she bumps them off.'

Surrender conditions

A massive police manhunt was begun and a price of over $10,000 (around £23,000 today) was put on Phoolan's head, but for two years she eluded capture. Anxious to avoid a caste war, the government of Indira Gandhi eventually decided to negotiate.

By 1983 Phoolan was ill and many of her men had been killed, so she agreed to surrender – but only in the state of Madhya Pradesh; not in Uttar Pradesh where she feared she would be killed. Her conditions for surrender were that she would lay down her arms before a picture of Mahatma Gandhi and the goddess Durga, not the police; the only officials present were to be the chief minister of Madhya Pradesh and the superintendent of police, who was to be unarmed; Phoolan was to be tried in a special court; she would not be subjected to the death penalty and no member of her gang would serve more than eight years in jail; her beloved younger brother, then 14, was to be given a government job; her father's land taken by her cousin was to be returned to him; and her entire family, including the family cow and goat, were to be resettled on government land in Madhya Pradesh.

The surrender was to take place at a lavish ceremony in the village of Bhind. A crowd of 8,000 turned out for the occasion, including 70 foreign journalists from New Delhi and an equal number of Indian journalists, along with human rights officials, feminists and socialites, though none of them knew what Phoolan looked like. Not even the police had a photograph of her.

When Phoolan arrived, she was a slip of a girl – less than 5ft (1.50 m) tall – with high cheekbones, a full flat nose and slit eyes. She was dressed in a khaki police superintendent's uniform and a bright red shawl and wore a red bandanna on her head. A .315 Mauser hung from her shoulder, a long curved dagger was tucked into her belt and a bandolier covered her chest. On her wrist was a silver bangle, a religious symbol of the Sikh faith, and in the breast pocket of her police uniform she carried a small silver figurine of Durga.

She climbed the wooden steps of a 23-foot-high (7 m) dais, shaded by an awning of red, green and yellow cloth, while Hindi film music blasted over a public-address system. After kneeling in homage to the chief minister of Madhya Pradesh, Arjun Singh, she turned towards the crowd and raised her rifle above her head. Then she folded her hands in the traditional gesture of greeting and lowered her eyes. The crowd roared its approval.

Movie of life story

Phoolan Devi was then held in prison for eight years without trial.

'I rotted in jail,' she said. 'Everyone simply forgot that I was there. Indira Gandhi, who agreed to my terms, was dead. The chief minister of Madhya Pradesh had been assigned to another state. I had no money, and I couldn't get legal aid.'

Eventually a new low-caste chief minister was elected in Uttar Pradesh, where the St Valentine's Day Massacre had occurred. The charges against Phoolan were dropped and she was released in 1994. That year, the movie *Bandit Queen* – based on the book *India's Bandit Queen: The True Story of Phoolan Devi*, by the Indian author Mala Sen – was premiered at the Cannes Film Festival. Phoolan fiercely disputed the accuracy of the film and fought to get it banned, even threatening to immolate herself outside a cinema if it was not withdrawn. She filed lawsuits in an attempt to keep it out of the cinemas, on the grounds that it was an unauthorized invasion of her privacy.

'It's simply not the story of my life, so how can they claim it is?' she said. 'How can they say "This is a true story" when my cousin Maiyadin, the major nemesis of my life, isn't even in the film? There's absolutely no mention of my family's land dispute. In the film I'm portrayed as a snivelling woman, always in tears, who never took a conscious decision in her life. I'm simply shown as being raped, over and over again.'

When journalist Mary Anne Weaver from *Atlantic* magazine, who interviewed her, pointed out that she *was* raped, she protested, saying:

> You can call it rape in your fancy language. Do you have any idea what it's like to live in a village in India? What you call rape, that kind of thing happens to poor women in the villages every day. It is assumed that the daughters of the poor are for the use of the rich. They assume that we're their property. In the villages the poor have no toilets, so we must go to the fields, and the moment we arrive, the rich lay us there; we can't cut the grass or tend to our crops without being accosted by them. We are the property of the rich.

Eventually Phoolan accepted a monetary settlement from the producers. Meanwhile, the film brought her international recognition. It also caused problems for the Indian censor because of its violent rape scenes, nudity and depiction of sensitive political issues, though an outright ban was eventually lifted. Nevertheless, it won several accolades at the National Film Awards in India, including Best Feature Film in Hindi.

Revenge killing

Two years later Phoolan Devi was elected MP for the constituency of Mirzapur in Uttar Pradesh as a champion of women, the poor and the downtrodden, styling herself the Gandhi of Mirzapur. She then married a wealthy estate agent, whom she referred to as 'my wife'. In 2001, she was shot by three masked men outside her bungalow in Delhi. With three bullets in her head and two in her body she was declared dead on arrival at the hospital. The chief suspect, Sher Singh Rana, surrendered to the police, saying he had killed her in revenge for the Behmai massacre. In 2014, he was sentenced to life imprisonment.

CHAPTER 22

DELFINA AND MARÍA DE JESÚS GONZÁLEZ

DELFINA AND MARÍA de Jesús González Valenzuela were known in Mexico by the nickname 'Las Poquianchis'. They were thought to have killed around 110 people, making them the 'most prolific murder partnership', according to Guinness World Records. They were all the more notorious for forcing young girls into prostitution in a chain of brothels they owned, including one described by inmates as a 'concentration camp'. Its name was Rancho Loma del Ángel.

Bars-cum-brothels

Delfina and María de Jesús González Valenzuela, along with their sisters María del Carmen and María Luisa, were born into poverty in El Salto, Jalisco in western Mexico in the early 1900s. Their father, Isidro Torres, a violent man, was a rural policeman under the hard-line president Portfirio Díaz. He forbade his daughters to wear make-up or sexy clothing and they were not to have boyfriends. If they disobeyed him, he was not above throwing them into jail. The family fortunes did not improve after he shot a man in an argument. He then took them all to live in the small village of San Francisco del

Rincón, called San Pancho by the locals, in the neighbouring state of Guanajuato.

To escape poverty and the strictures of their father, the sisters opened a bar. When this was not a success, they branched out into prostitution, running a chain of bar-cum-brothels in Jalisco, Guanajuato and Querétaro. These operated with impunity, because they paid off the authorities and offered sexual services to officials. One of their enterprises was a saloon bought from a gay man called 'El Poquianchi' and the name Poquianchis, which they hated, stuck.

Few girls survived

The González sisters began recruiting girls by putting small ads asking for maids in local newspapers. Women who responded were promised a good job with good pay, but in fact they would be forced into prostitution. Others would simply be kidnapped. Attractive girls would either be sold on to other madams for $40 to $80 (perhaps £275–£550/$360–$725 today) or sent to work in the sisters' own brothels. There they would be imprisoned and any who resisted were beaten and tortured. They were given a simple choice – they either worked or died. To make them easier to handle, girls were forced into heroin or cocaine addiction.

Girls who got pregnant were given an abortion by the simple expedient of hanging them up by the hands and beating them around the belly until they miscarried. At Rancho Loma del Ángel particularly, girls were forced to survive on meagre helpings of tortillas and beans. When they lost their looks and no longer attracted clients, they were beaten to death or starved. Few lasted longer than five years.

Contracting a sexually transmitted disease carried a death sentence and clients carrying large amounts of cash were also killed. The bodies were dumped into mass graves along with aborted foetuses, or buried in shallow graves to be disinterred later and burned.

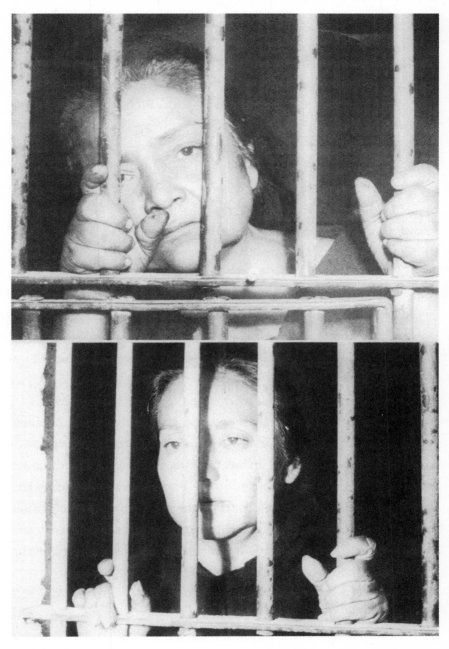

Delfina González Valenzuela, 53, (top) and Maria de Jesus González Valenzuela, 39, behind bars in the San Francisco del Rincon jail. The sisters were convicted of first degree murder, slavery and other crimes.

As the business expanded, the sisters hired former army captain Hermenegildo 'The Black Eagle' Zuniga and Estrada 'The Executioner' Bocanegra to kidnap new girls. Virgins were particularly prized as clients were willing to pay more money for them. Delfina's son Ramon 'El Tepo' Torres was also on hand to keep the girls in line, making sure the business was enormously profitable.

Sisters' downfall

Accounts of the sisters' downfall differ. One version has it that in 1963 El Tepo got into an argument with a policeman, who shot him dead inside one of their brothels. The police closed the establishment down and Delfina then ordered her lover Hermenegildo Zuniga to track down and kill the policeman who had killed her son. This sparked a war between the police and the brothel owners and in the ensuing struggle another procuress named Josefina Gutiérrez was picked up on suspicion of kidnapping young girls in the Guanajuato area. To secure her own freedom, she informed on the González sisters.

In another version, three of the sex slaves in Rancho Loma del Ángel escaped and Zuniga and his accomplices scoured the countryside to kill them. One of them, Catalina Ortega, found her way back home to the city of Leon, Guanajuato where her mother took her to the police station to file charges. Luckily the police there were not on the sisters' payroll. Though Catalina's story was hard to credit, she showed clear signs of malnutrition and abuse, so the police obtained a search warrant for Rancho Loma del Ángel.

Mass graves

On 14 January 1964, the ranch was raided and the police found a dozen emaciated women being held in filthy conditions. As police and reporters explored the premises, the girls told them where they would find bodies. Zuniga and his men were forced to excavate the graves and they unearthed the decomposed bodies of 80 women, 11 men and an unknown number of infants and foetuses. Delfina and María de Jesús fled, but were caught trying to sell their possessions so they could skip the country.

Still dressed in black, as they were mourning El Tepo, they were brought back to the ranch to face angry villagers who wanted them lynched. But the sisters denied any wrongdoing. They had simply been providing a service, they said, and Delfina insisted they were not responsible for any of the deaths.

'The little dead ones died all by themselves,' she declared. 'Maybe the food did not agree with them.'

Another of the sisters, María Luisa González, aka 'Eva the Leggy One', ran a separate operation, but fearing that she might be lynched she turned herself in at a Mexico City police station. The fourth sister, María del Carmen, had already died of cancer and was not implicated.

Died in jail

As well as being charged with rape, murder and extortion, the three sisters were also accused of corrupting and bribing the government officials who frequented their bars and brothels. In a chaotic trial, the sisters exchanged insults at the top of their voices. They were convicted and sentenced to 40 years in jail, the maximum sentence in Mexico.

Terrified that she would be murdered in jail, Delfina went mad and was accidentally killed when a workman making repairs dropped a bucket of cement on her head. María Luisa died alone in her cell on 19 November 1984, after 20 years in jail. Her body was found the following day, already half-eaten by rats. María de Jesús, the youngest of the sisters, was eventually released and legend has it that she married a 64-year-old man she had met in prison and died of old age in the mid-1990s.

In 2002, workers excavating the land for a new housing development in Purísima del Rincón, Guanajuato, near the Loma del Ángel ranch, found around 20 skeletons in a pit. The authorities concluded that these belonged to other victims of Las Poquianchis, and were probably buried there in the 1950s or 1960s. This would raise the sisters' death toll to over 110.

CHAPTER 23

RHONDA BELLE MARTIN

RHONDA BELLE MARTIN was known as Little Mrs Arsenic. In 1956, the 49-year-old waitress in Montgomery, Alabama, admitted murdering two husbands, her mother and three of her children – though she denied killing another two of her children who died in mysterious circumstances. She was caught because her attempt to kill her fifth husband – the son of her poisoned fourth husband – failed, which allowed doctors to gather evidence. The prosecution maintained that she had committed the murders in order to claim on the insurance policies she had taken out on all of her victims, but the amounts were trivial, barely covering the cost of burial. Even Rhonda could not find any other explanation for her crimes.

Cotton poison in milk

Born in Alabama in 1907, Rhonda Martin, née Thomley, was eager to have children, but her first marriage to W.R. Alderman in 1922 proved fruitless. They divorced in 1926 and two years later she married railwayman George W. Garrett. Their first child, Adelaide, Rhonda said, was 'born afflicted'.

'I loved her terribly,' she said. 'I sat over her and nursed her day and night for the three years and four months she lived.' She died, ostensibly of pneumonia. 'When she died, it could have done something to me . . . I don't know,' Rhonda went on, trying to make sense of her life as she waited on Death Row.

Her next child was Emogene, who was just two and a half years old when she died.

'The idea of poison never did enter my head until my stepfather got to talking about it,' Rhonda said. 'He told us there was a corn crib out in the field. And he told us not to go near the crib or let the children near it, because he told us what was in there – some white powder, some cotton poison he used in the field. He told us not to go near it.'

Nevertheless, she went and got some and put it in Emogene's milk. Two hours later, the child had convulsions.

'We rushed her to the hospital and I told them, because she died so quick, I wondered if she hadn't got poisoned,' Rhonda said.

She was told that Emogene's organs had been sent to the state toxicology and crime investigation laboratory at Auburn. But even though the matter was in the hands of the coroner, no further action was taken.

Ant poison all round

The next person to die was her husband George Garrett.

'He was the father of all my girls and the one I was happiest with,' she said. 'I put ant poison in his whisky – two or three teaspoonfuls, I reckon – and he died a little after Emogene.'

Their daughter Carolyn died the following year, aged six, after Rhonda put ant poison in her milk.

'I had to give it to her two or three times,' she said. 'Carolyn was awfully smart and pretty as a picture. It was her first year at school, and her teacher was so proud of her . . . he came and told me how bright she was.'

Next came 11-year-old Ellyn.

'But she was sickly . . . had some kind of paralysis, before I give it to her. We had to bury her about three years after Carolyn.'

Judith Garrett also died, aged one, but Rhonda denied killing her. However, she admitted killing her own mother when she was living with her.

'I was devoted to Mama,' she said. 'Then it came over me again, and I gave the ant poison to Mama and she died.'

'Loved and respected' victim

In the meantime, Rhonda married Talmadge John Gipson, but the marriage lasted less than a year and he escaped with his life. She married her fourth husband Claude C. Martin in 1950. A year after they were married, he became gravely ill, suffering severe abdominal pain and vomiting frequently. She had put ant poison in his coffee on three or four occasions. Doctors thought it was a virus, but there was nothing they could do for him and after several weeks of intense pain he died.

'I was good to him before he died,' Rhonda said. 'I took him to the hospital and stayed with him every minute. I really cared for him good. I'd help him get in and out of the car when he got so he couldn't even walk. But there was something wrong somewhere. I don't know *why* I didn't tell all those doctors what was really the matter with Claude.'

As with George Garrett, she had been happy with Claude Martin before she killed him.

'I loved and respected him,' she said. 'He was a good man. He didn't drink and he didn't smoke. And after I married him I never drank or smoked while he was alive. And I quit work at the glass factory so I could stay at home and be a mother to his three growing-up daughters. I didn't want to set a bad example before the girls . . .'

She would even accompany Claude to put flowers on his first wife's grave.

'I couldn't have been a better nurse to Claude after he got sick from the poison in his coffee,' she said. 'When he began hurting and moaning and would ask me to rub him I'd do it like I did for all the rest of 'em. And I'd get him a hot water bottle or anything he wanted.'

When he died, she had his first wife's body moved so that they could lie side by side.

'I thought he'd like that,' she said. 'I wanted it for him.'

Marries stepson

Eight months after Claude's death, Mrs Martin married her stepson Ronald C. Martin, 21 years her junior.

'When Bud's daddy – I called Ronald Bud – was on his death bed he asked Bud to see I was well taken care of,' she explained. 'I was nice to Bud, treated him like a mother, and it wasn't long before he asked me to marry him.'

Whether this union was incestuous was argued over later in court. Mrs Martin told them:

> At first I told him I didn't think it was right. There was too much difference in our ages and he needed a young wife. But he said, no, he'd never seen a woman before that he wanted to marry and he'd have asked me to marry him even if his daddy hadn't asked him that. So I married him. He didn't seem to care much for people of his own age and we got along fine. We both like to fish. We bought a motor and a boat and I was a good wife to him in every way.

However, after four years of marriage Ronald began to suffer from the same mysterious illness that had killed his father and a year later he became paralysed from the waist down.

'I put it in his coffee several times the month before that,' she said. 'Why didn't I tell the doctors what was the matter with him? That's what I want to know! Why didn't I tell them?'

Confesses to murder spree

In an attempt to find a diagnosis, doctors analysed a sample of his hair and found arsenic. When the police began to investigate Rhonda's background, they found that those around her died with astonishing frequency and they arrested her. For three or four days she denied everything, but when they told her that they had dug up Claude Martin and were going to dig up the others, she confessed to a 17-year murder spree.

'Seems like something suddenly came over me and I just had to let it all go,' she said. 'Nobody but my God knows what I went through holding it all back all these years, and what a relief it was to tell it.'

A psychiatrist who examined her came up with some theories.

'He told me I killed him [Claude Martin] so I could marry his son,' said Rhonda. 'That wasn't so, because Ronald was off in the navy then and I didn't know anything about him. He told me I killed people to get rid of responsibility, and I don't think that was so, either.'

She stood trial only for the murder of her fourth husband, Claude Martin. Her plea of insanity failed, with the prosecution arguing that she had deliberately put arsenic in her husband's coffee to 'collect some paltry amount of insurance and to get him out of the way so she could marry his son'. She was convicted and sentenced to death.

Under Alabama's state law, the case automatically went to appeal at the state's Supreme Court. There it was argued that Rhonda's confession was inadmissible because she had also admitted committing incest by marrying her stepson. This was a felony and was not part of the case being tried, so the confession could not be used in evidence. But the Supreme Court judged that as Claude Martin was dead at the time of Rhonda's marriage to Ronald – and she and Mr Martin senior had no children – the marriage was not incestuous, so the confession was admissible.

On Death Row, Rhonda Belle Martin was interviewed by journalist Allen Rankin, who asked her how her last husband, Ronald Martin, felt about her then.

'The last letter I had from him he told me he loves me just as much as he ever did. That he was just sorry there wasn't something more that he could do to help me,' she said. 'Bud's getting better, I hope and pray to God! The last letter I got from him he said he was walking without a stick now. But he said his hands weren't getting better as fast as his feet. He still can't hardly write yet.'

Never intended to kill

Asked why she felt the compulsion to kill, she answered in tears:

> I tell you I never intended to kill anybody! I just wanted to love them, to nurse them, to take care of them! I love them! I loved them all, don't you understand? The ones I done it to were the ones I was closest to, the ones I loved the best! Once they were sick I took the very best care of them I could. It would break my heart to see them suffer, to hear them cry out, 'Mama, it hurts so! Please help me!'

She also insisted that she gave everyone she had killed a nice funeral and put flowers on their graves every week. Nor did she have nightmares about what she had done – 'always pleasant dreams . . . dreams back with Mama or George or Claude or my little girls all alive'.

Execution

After a last meal of hamburger, mashed potatoes, cinnamon roll and coffee, Rhonda Belle Martin walked into the death chamber wearing a new black-and-white dress she had made and her wedding ring. A few minutes after midnight on 11 October 1956, she was strapped into the electric chair and was asked if she had anything to say. She just shook her head. The switch was then thrown, but it was found that the electrodes had not been plugged in. Three minutes later, she was given 2,200 volts of electricity. She stiffened and soon afterwards was pronounced dead.

Later, a note was found in her cell which read:

At my death, whether it be a natural death or otherwise, I want my body to be given to some scientific institution to be used as they see fit, but especially to see if someone can find out why I committed the crimes I have committed. I can't understand it, for I had no reason whatsoever. There is definitely something wrong. Can't someone find it and save someone else the agony I have been through?

CHAPTER 24

MARGARET JAMES

ON 18 JUNE 2004, 5 miles (8 km) off Black Head on the Lizard Peninsula in Cornwall, England, the crew of the fishing boat *Clairvoyant* hauled in a strange catch. It was the half-naked body of a middle-aged man. They dragged the corpse on board and landed it at Falmouth Docks.

A media appeal resulted in him being identified as 56-year-old Peter Solheim, who lived in Carnkie. The previous year he had become a parish councillor for Budock Water, the village where he grew up and where his mother still lived, 9 miles (14 km) away on the outskirts of Falmouth. A post-mortem established that the immediate cause of death was drowning – at least, that was what was released to the press.

In fact, he had suffered 18 separate injuries, including four deep gashes to the head. It was thought at first that these had been caused by a boat's propeller, but the pathologist determined that they had been made by an axe or machete. There was also extensive bruising to his back and chest and he had a broken kneecap and broken ribs, along with a severed big toe. Grazing to the buttocks seemed to indicate that he had been dragged along the ground and there was a high level of the sedative Lorazepam in his blood. None of this was consistent with a boating accident.

Solheim had still been alive when he hit the water. Unable to help himself, he had then drowned. Clearly this was a murder inquiry. The pathologist raised the possibility that Solheim had been kept prisoner for two days and tortured, before being dragged across some rough ground and dumped in the sea.

Girlfriend interviewed

The police discovered that he had a girlfriend, 56-year-old Margaret James, who lived in a former coastguard's cottage outside Porthoustock, 15 miles (24 km) from his home and just 4 miles (6.5 km) from Black Head. She said the last time she had seen Peter was on 16 June, when she had driven him to Mylor Harbour, where he was meeting a friend called Charlie. The two men were setting out on a boat trip together.

Asked why she had not reported Peter missing, she explained that she expected him to stay out at sea for some time. However, Solheim's boat, a 12ft (3.7 m) dinghy called the *Izzwizz*, was not equipped for night fishing. She said she believed that Charlie had a bigger boat, which the two men planned to use for longer fishing trips to France or Spain. But she did not know Charlie's surname, nor did she have a contact number. Indeed, she knew nothing more about him. Working from an eight-man incident room in Falmouth Police Station, the police set about trying to trace him, amid fears that a second man had been lost at sea.

Nevertheless, the detectives who had interviewed Margaret James had their doubts. She was strangely unperturbed about the death of her boyfriend of eight or nine years and indifferent to the suffering he had clearly undergone. Not only that but she was also

Falmouth where the body of Peter Solheim was brought back to shore.

vague on details, leading the police to suspect that she was not telling them everything she knew.

Suspicious factors

On 17 June the *Izzwizz* had been found in Mylor Harbour, with the keys still in the ignition. The coastguard was asked whether Solheim could have fallen from the *Izzwizz* and then floated out to sea while the boat drifted back into the harbour. A study of the tides showed that this was impossible.

At the time, Detective Inspector Neil Best said: 'We have consulted experts on winds and tides and they have told us they were not consistent with the resultant positions of the boat and the body, which was 13 miles (21 km) from Mylor Harbour. When you put all these factors together, we have to conclude that this has really gone beyond an unexplained death.'

Either Solheim had set sail on another boat or someone had sailed the *Izzwizz* back to port after his body had been dumped.

Meets Margaret James

The police began to look into the background of Peter Solheim to see if they could find any motive for his murder. Solheim's father, a Norwegian, was the chief engineer on a whaler, so he had often been away at sea. As a result, Peter had largely been brought up by his mother. Although he learned to sail, he had no ambition to follow his father into a life at sea. However, he had inherited his father's engineering skills and worked in the printing industry mending machinery, though he had retired at the time of his death.

In 1971, he married a clerk named Jean Poley and they had two children. However, Solheim showed symptoms of being bipolar and they divorced. His daughter Lisa said that the separation changed him. He became angry and struggled to rein in his temper. After a row, he broke off relations with his children.

He comforted himself in the arms of other women, answering numerous lonely hearts ads. In 1995 he answered one from Margaret James, a widow who had struggled to raise two children alone. Her husband had been killed in a fire and an insurance claim had allowed her to buy the coastguard's cottage.

Unfaithful

In Porthoustock she was seen as an eccentric who swam naked and walked barefoot whatever the weather. She was also a vegan who was considered to be a hippy and some said that she kept her house in a filthy condition. However, she looked after her elderly mother and was on good terms with her daughter Lucy and her grandchildren.

At their first meeting, Solheim turned up at her home with a bunch of flowers. The relationship was passionate – she told the police that they were soon 'at it like rabbits'. However, she quickly discovered that Solheim had no intention of being faithful.

He developed an interest in witchcraft and she joined him in the rituals and celebrations, but even though Margaret was with him he made obvious overtures to other women, boasting of his sexual prowess. He soon veered towards the dark side of witchcraft, claiming to be channelling Thor, the hammer-wielding Germanic god. He also renamed his house Valhalla, the Norse refuge for slain warriors. Some of the covens he belonged to asked him to leave.

After he had left a pagan sect to experiment in the occult on his own, a member said:

> It became clear he wanted to go into areas everyone else felt uncomfortable with. He started to get involved with Satanism

and liked to go off and perform rituals by himself. He was always making knives and swords. We became really worried about him. Once, he tried to perform black magic spells on two other people. It really upset them. I don't know what his rituals involved, but he'd always do them on his own. Eventually, he stopped coming to our gatherings.

Long-running affair

Margaret tried to take a relaxed hippy view of his infidelity, but she was clearly racked with jealousy. She spied on him and even broke into his home, where she discovered women's underwear that he kept as trophies, along with various potions and a voodoo doll.

Solheim made no effort to hide his unfaithfulness, but he still managed to convince Margaret that his relationship with her was the most important thing in his life. However, this was not true because he had been pursuing a long-running affair with three-time divorcee Jean Knowles that had gone on for 20 years. They met up for sex three or four times a month. Margaret warned Jean to stay away from Solheim, but the affair continued anyway.

Margaret may have been intimidated by Solheim's volatile temper. He maintained feuds with his neighbours and fired guns in his garden. When following up villagers' complaints, the police were advised to use caution when dealing with him. At his home, they found a hoard of knives and antique guns, some of which were unlicensed.

As a councillor he had a passion for the environment, but he blamed periodic flooding on 'river spirits'. He also cultivated a dislike of outsiders. Even people who had moved into the area decades earlier could not be considered properly Cornish, he said.

Solheim's missing money

One reason why Margaret put up with Solheim was money. Ostensibly she lived on a widow's pension of £327 ($430) a month while Solheim was living on a disability allowance. However, he supplemented this by selling antique firearms and pornography and it was well known that he kept large amounts of cash about the house. When the police searched his home after his death, though, his safe was missing and they found just £20 ($26).

They then looked into Margaret James' finances and found that she had an ISA worth over £7,000 ($9250), £15,270 ($20,000) in a National Savings account, a £12,564 ($16,000) capital bond, £671 ($880) in a dormant Barclays account, £650-worth ($860) of premium bonds and £71,725 ($95,000) invested under her daughter's name. Another £900 ($,1200) in cash was found under her mattress, along with £24,000 ($31,700) at a house in nearby Helston which belonged to her mother.

The money, it seems, had come from Solheim. Once she had found £900 ($1,200) in a book in his house. As they were leaving she made an excuse to go back. She then hid the money in her skirt and left a fanlight open, so it would look as if he had been burgled if he noticed the money was gone.

Texts sent from dead man

Margaret experimented with potions and incantations that would make Solheim hers exclusively, but these failed. Instead, he decided to marry Jean and began renovating his mother's old house for them to live in. Margaret, the younger of the two women, was incensed and her experiments with potions turned to poisons.

Realizing that he was going to have a problem with Margaret, Solheim asked Jean not to wear the engagement ring he had bought her. The police then noticed that on 15 June, the day before he went missing, he had written on a calendar in his home: 'Secret's found out.'

After 16 June, both Jean and Margaret continued to receive texts from Solheim, saying that he was meeting Charlie. Some even arrived after his body was lying in the morgue at Falmouth. The texts to Jean mentioned 'Margaret', but Solheim always referred to Margaret as 'M' and latterly 'it'. They were also being transmitted via the mobile mast at St Keverne, which was the nearest one to Margaret's mother's home.

Conspiracy to murder

The police thought it unlikely that Margaret, who was only a small woman, could have struck down Solheim and then manhandled his body into the boat and dumped him at sea, so they began to look for an accomplice.

Interviewing Stanley Reeves, her former son-in-law and the father of her two grandchildren, the police learned that some three years earlier Margaret had asked him whether he knew of anyone who could 'get rid of' Solheim. The speculation was that she had used some of Solheim's money to pay someone to help her kill him. However, in February 2005, Margaret James alone was charged with murder and conspiracy to murder.

In Truro Crown Court, her ex-son-in-law testified that she had asked him to find someone to kill Solheim, asking how much it would cost. She had also discussed the possibility of poisoning him. Asked why he had not gone to the police, he said he thought it best to warn Solheim directly.

All this looked bad for Margaret James. The case was made that she rendered Solheim defenceless by adding a powerful sedative to the food she had prepared for him and then imprisoned him, even tearing a ring, a gift from Jean, from his finger. However, as she remained silent it was impossible to prove conclusively that she had done so – or even that she was present if it had been done by someone else.

After the prosecution had made its case, Judge Graham Cottle told the jury:

> The prosecution, in order to succeed, have to prove either that the defendant alone murdered Solheim or that she played an actual part in his murder. There is, in my judgement, and it is my judgement as a matter of law, insufficient evidence for either of these conclusions safely to be drawn. It therefore follows that when you are returning your verdict on the conspiracy charge you will on my direction return a verdict of not guilty in relation to the charge of murder. Hereafter you will be considering the conspiracy charge alone.

Four weeks later, the jury returned a verdict of guilty on the conspiracy charge, finding that she had plotted to murder Peter Solheim. Imposing a sentence of 20 years, Judge Cottle said:

> It was you who wanted him dead and you who masterminded and orchestrated the events which culminated in his death. I have no doubt at all that the arrangement for his abduction, torture and disposal were of your making. And what you orchestrated was a horrific and slow death.

He added:

> I have had an extensive opportunity to observe you during this trial which has lasted over ten weeks. I have had the opportunity to see you give evidence and heard from you over a period of several days – you are a consummate actress, the

performance demonstrated your ability to lie with apparent conviction but clearly you experience no remorse for what you did.

In 2012, during a court case involving two other Satanists convicted of paedophilia, Solheim was accused of being part of a ring who sexually abused young girls as part of their rituals, terrifying their victims with hooded robes and daggers. Lead investigator Detective Constable Rick Milburn said: 'It was truly horrific abuse, the worst my officers and myself have ever seen.'

But then, Solheim had already paid with his life.

CHAPTER 25

MARGARET 'BILL' ALLEN

IN 1906, MARGARET ALLEN was born the 20th of 22 children and suffered from what is now known as gender dysphoria, a condition not recognized until the 1980s. That is, while she was biologically a female, she felt herself to be a male. In 1935, at the age of 29, she claimed to have had a sex-change operation, turning her from a woman into a man, though that procedure was not carried out for the first time until 1946.

Dressed in men's clothes

Identifying herself as Bill, she had her hair cropped, dressed in men's clothes and worked on labouring jobs traditionally the preserve of men in pre-war Britain – delivering coal, painting and decorating, and doing building work. She also hung out with men in the pubs and working-men's clubs of her hometown of Rawtenstall in Lancashire. When men were called up during World War II, she took a job at the post office and from July 1942 to June 1946 she worked as a bus conductor with the Rawtenstall Motor Corporation. Though she was helpful, especially to the elderly and infirm, there were outbursts of masculine violence and she abused passengers. She quit after four years, seemingly due to ill health.

Badly affected by her mother's death in 1943, she became withdrawn and depressed, eating badly and smoking and drinking to excess. She had invested her savings in a run-down house that had once been a police cottage in the Bacup district of Rawtenstall. The place was filthy, it was infested with lice and she sold the gas cooker to pay her bills. In 1945, she was treated for dizziness and vertigo and was diagnosed with clinical depression. Three years later, she lost a short-lived job in a slipper factory and began to undergo the menopause.

Only friend

Bill Allen had one friend in the world, Mrs Annie Cook, whom she had met in 1946. Existing on the meagre benefits available at the time, Allen tried to kill herself twice. Annie once found her with a gas tube in her mouth.

At Whitsun in 1948 they took a short holiday in Blackpool, where Bill registered as Mr Allen. Annie was attractive and feminine and Bill made a pass at her, but Annie was not responsive and their relationship cooled for a while.

Battered to death

Bill then struck up an acquaintanceship with 68-year-old Nancy Chadwick, known locally as 'Old Nancy', who read fortunes using cards and tea leaves. She was widowed in 1921 and since 1938 had kept house for an elderly gentleman named Paddy Whittaker. Otherwise she hung out in parks and bus shelters, begging for cups of tea. But she was not poor. Previously she had kept house for a stonemason, who left her four houses, bringing in a healthy income from rents. Her comparative affluence was well known and had led to her being robbed two years earlier.

Bus driver Herbert Beaumont reported seeing Mrs Chadwick's dead body at the corner of Fallbarn Close and Bacup Road, Rawtenstall's main street, a few feet from Allen's home, at 3.35 a.m. on 29 August 1948. Another bus driver named Arthur Marshall told police the body had not been there when he passed 15 minutes earlier. Her coat had been pulled up over her head, hiding extensive injuries. At first, she appeared to be the victim of a traffic accident, but a post-mortem carried out by Dr Gilbert Bailey of Blackburn determined that her wounds had been made with the spike of the type of hammer used to break up coal. In other words, she had been battered to death. The local paper, the *Bacup Times*, reported that this was the first murder in Rawtenstall in living memory. Scotland Yard sent Detective Chief Inspector Stevens and the search for the murder weapon began.

Murder confession

Mrs Chadwick was thought to carry large amounts of money in her handbag, which was missing. As the investigation of Chadwick's murder continued, Allen took an inordinate interest. When the police were searching the area, she pointed out Mrs Chadwick's bag floating in the River Irwell nearby. It was recovered, but there was no money in it.

Allen also boasted in pubs that she had been the last person to see Mrs Chadwick alive and roundly condemned her for sitting on a public bench counting her money. When the police went to Allen's house to interview her, they found blood on the walls and inside the front door, along with rags and ashes used to clean the floor, and she freely confessed to the murder.

'I'll tell you all about it,' she said, leading them to the coal cellar. 'That's where I put her. I didn't actually do it for the money. I was in one of my funny moods.'

Although Mrs Chadwick was a near neighbour, the two women had never got on. The dispute that day seems to have been about

sugar, which was still rationed post-war. It was also thought that
Allen had borrowed money from Mrs Chadwick. She confessed to the
police, saying:

> I was coming out of the house on Saturday morning at about
> 9.30 and Mrs Chadwick came round the corner. She asked me
> was this where I lived and could she come in? I was in a nervy
> mood and she just seemed to get on my nerves, although she
> had not said anything. I told her to go and she could see me
> some time else. But she seemed to insist on coming in. I just
> happened to look around and saw the hammer in the kitchen.
> At this time we were talking inside the kitchen with the front
> door shut. On the spur of the moment I hit her with the
> hammer. She gave a loud shout and that seemed to start me
> off more. I hit her a few times, but I don't know how many. I
> pulled her body into my coal house.

After putting Mrs Chadwick's body in the coal cellar, she threw her
bag and the hammer into the Irwell and then she went to the Food
Office with Mrs Cook. They had a drink at the nearby Ashworth Arms
and Allen then visited her sister, returning to the pub that evening.
During the night, she decided to dispose of the corpse in the river,
but it was too heavy and rigid from rigor mortis to drag that far, so
she abandoned it in the street. And Mrs Chadwick was not the only
victim. Eighty-two-year-old Paddy Whittaker was so upset by her
death that he drowned himself.

Trial

The trial lasted just five hours. Allen wore a suit and tie in the dock,
which did her no favours with a 1940s jury. Her defence was insanity,

but the confession she had given when she was arrested was clear and concise, undermining her insanity plea. She failed to go into the witness box in her own defence. There was no allegation that she had been provoked and no hint of regret.

The jury took just 15 minutes to find her guilty, with no recommendation of mercy, so the judge was obliged to pass a sentence of death. Mrs Cook made an attempt to get up a petition for a reprieve and it was signed by just 162 people. She was the only one to visit Allen in prison. While the Home Secretary James Chuter Ede was personally opposed to the death penalty, he could find no grounds on which to commute the sentence and Allen did not appeal, though she made two requests – that she should meet Annie Cook alone and that the execution be postponed until after Mrs Cook's birthday. Both were denied.

When Mrs Cook made her last supervised visit before she was hanged, Allen said: 'I'm going to have chicken for dinner and a few bottles before they put the rope around my neck. It would help if I could cry, but my manhood holds back my tears.'

Mrs Cook told the press: 'I don't think Allen ever realized the seriousness of her position. She seemed to have nerves of iron.'

Faced death like a man

In fact, her last meal was a plate of scrambled eggs. Forced to quit her male attire for a striped prison dress for the execution, she grew annoyed and kicked over the tray, saying: 'I don't want it and no one else is going to enjoy it.'

She walked to the scaffold in Strangeways jail in Manchester on 12 January 1949 without making a final statement and was hanged by public executioner Albert Pierrepoint. The Reverend Arthur Walker, the chaplain at Strangeways, witnessed the event. He said:

She was a woman with plenty of grit and she faced it as a man would and I felt the whole thing was bestial and brutal. She was well prepared and behaved like a man. In fact she had more guts than most men I have seen. A prison official has told me that he has never felt fit since the thing happened and it happened over 12 months ago.

At the time of the execution, Annie Cook stood on the corner of Bacup Road and Kay Road where they had so often met. Comforted by her sister, she asked: 'Why did she have to die when so many others were reprieved?'

The Reverend Walker told a Royal Commission on Capital Punishment the following year that no woman should be hanged.

'If the state recognized the physical and mental differences between the sexes and refused to flog women then the more cruel punishment of hanging should be abolished,' he said.

CHAPTER 26

FLORENCE RANSOM

IT WAS 48-YEAR-OLD Mrs Dorothy Sanders Fisher's custom to take tea on Tuesdays with her 83-year-old mother, Mrs Gibbs, when her housekeeper was out. But on 9 July 1940 she did not turn up. When Mrs Gibbs's housekeeper returned, she phoned Dorothy Fisher's home, 'Crittenden', in the English village of Matfield, Kent, but got no reply.

Mrs Gibbs then sent her gardener J.D. Leury to investigate. He found the body of Charlotte Saunders, Dorothy Fisher's 47-year-old maid, in the front garden. She had sustained terrible head injuries. He immediately called the police and later described what had taken place:

> Mrs Fisher or her daughters always used to call on Mrs Gibbs when Mrs Gibbs's housekeeper was away. On Tuesday Mrs Gibbs's housekeeper had gone to a meeting at Brenchley, and Mrs Gibbs was expecting Mrs Fisher to call. She waited for some time for Mrs Fisher to come but she did not arrive, and when Mrs Gibbs's housekeeper returned they became alarmed.

When I called at Mrs Gibbs's house, as I often used to do, they
asked me to go and find what had happened to Mrs Fisher so
I set off down the road. When I got inside the front gate I saw
the body of Miss Saunders lying in front of the house just off a
long path which leads to the front door. I immediately ran to
call the police, who were soon on the scene.

Arrested

A large squad under Superintendent Cook arrived to make what
investigations they could before it got dark. In the orchard nearby,
they found the bodies of Dorothy Fisher and her daughter Freda.
The police worked on the assumption that they were shot first and on
hearing the shots the maid ran out of the door of the house and was
struck down either by the butt of the gun or some other instrument.
A search of the grounds was made.

The peaceful village of Matfield in Kent.

At six o'clock that evening, an official statement was released at Tonbridge Police Station, saying:

> On the evening of July the 9th the three occupants of Crittenden House, Matfield, near Tonbridge, were found dead in the grounds of the house. The three deceased persons were Mrs D. Fisher aged 48, her daughter Freda aged 20 and Charlotte Saunders aged 47. The two former were killed by gunshot wounds and the latter by head injuries.

A villager told the *Kent & Sussex Courier*:

> The family always seemed to be a little mysterious. That was probably because they were reserved. Mrs Fisher would talk to you pleasantly but you felt that you could never get to know them. Nobody in the village had any idea what had transpired at the house until a large number of police swooped on the place in cars. Even then no thought was given to the possibility of such a dreadful tragedy. It has become a dreadful shock to the village although the family were not well known.

The following morning Scotland Yard's Flying Squad under Chief Inspector Peter Beveridge was on the scene. The house was in disorder, but nothing valuable was missing. A pond was dragged and the surrounding woodland combed and in these searches a white ox-skin glove was found. It belonged to Florence Ransom, the 34-year-old mistress of Dorothy Fisher's husband. She was promptly arrested.

Social climber

Florence Ransom and Lawrence Fisher, who was the editor of *Automobile Engineer*, lived together on a farm in Piddington, Oxfordshire, while his wife was living with their daughter in Matfield. This complicated arrangement had begun five or six years earlier when Lawrence Fisher was introduced to Florence Iris Ouida Ransom, then a 28-year-old red-headed beauty, at a party. The daughter of portrait painter Frederick Guilford, she was born in Preston, Lancashire, in 1904. She was known there as a vivacious girl, but the family broke up and, according to her own account, she travelled widely. However, the details of her travels were vague and she liked to be thought of as a mystery woman. Some people were informed that she was a changeling and her mother had been hired to take care of her, while others were told that she was upper class and her real name was Lady Iris Cornwallis-West. Lawrence Fisher was entirely taken in.

'I never enquired deeply about her past,' he said. 'But she gave me to understand she was a woman of gentle birth. She acted the part to perfection.'

At the age of 21 she married 22-year-old bookseller's warehouse clerk Douglas Ransom, but he died a few years later, leaving her to fend for herself. Pretty and sociable, she became a knowledgeable woman of the world and a social climber.

Moves to farm

With the knowledge of his wife, Fisher took her as his mistress, while Dorothy Fisher had a lover of her own, a Dane. Nevertheless, the Fishers continued to live together in the family home in Twickenham. Florence was a frequent visitor there, as was Dorothy Fisher's lover.

Lawrence Fisher then bought Carramore Farm in Piddington, near Bicester in Oxfordshire in 1938 and moved there. Masquerading as Mrs Fisher, Florence was installed as the manager of the 100-acre farm and doubled as Fisher's secretary. Florence then moved her mother, brother and sister-in-law into a cottage on the estate. Her mother was employed as her maid and her brother was a cowman, though Lawrence Fisher knew nothing of their relationship.

'It was a great shock to me when I learned that Mrs Guilford was her mother and that the cowkeeper on the farm was her brother,' he said. 'She always had an air of mystery about her.'

She was a woman of mystery to the local villagers too and kept herself aloof. Occasionally she would be seen riding in a pony and trap, but it was beneath her dignity to acknowledge their hellos. Even those she deigned to speak to found her unfathomable.

'She would talk for a long time about nothing in particular and contradict herself often,' a friend told the *Daily Mail*. 'She was always vague about her own history, saying merely that she had travelled a great deal. She always knew a great deal about any subject or place that cropped up in conversation.'

Generally, she was looked on with awe as a masterful woman, though her temper was sometimes uncontrollable. In fits of rage, she would fire the whole staff, only to withdraw their notice when she calmed down.

Plans shooting

In March 1940, the real Mrs Fisher and Freda moved into a cottage Lawrence Fisher had taken for them in Matfield. Their domestic arrangements seemed perfectly civilized, but tensions arose. When the Battle of Britain started, Kent found itself in the front line and Lawrence Fisher travelled down to Matfield frequently to make sure that his wife and daughter were safe. He also gave them money so they could employ a serving maid which, apparently, made Florence Ransom jealous. She was eager to marry Lawrence Fisher, but Dorothy Fisher refused her husband a divorce, so she cooked up a plot to eliminate her rival.

After checking the train timetables, she saw she could leave the farm in Oxfordshire after Lawrence had left for work in the morning and make it to Matfield and back before he returned. Then she learned to ride a bicycle, as she would have to cycle the 5 miles (8 km) from Tonbridge railway station to the cottage and back. She got her brother to teach her how to shoot, saying she wanted to shoot rabbits on the farm. Borrowing his .410 sporting shotgun, she bought 25 .410 cartridges in Oxford a week before her trip to Matfield.

She was seen on the train carrying a brown paper package, which the prosecution maintained contained the gun. It seems that Florence Ransom and Dorothy Fisher were on friendly terms, as Charlotte Saunders was preparing tea for them. What happened next is a matter of conjecture.

Escapes death penalty

The prosecution maintained that Florence Ransom had gone out shooting rabbits with Freda Fisher. Walking out into the orchard, Florence Ransom then shot the young woman in the back at close range. Dorothy Fisher saw what had happened and fled, but Ransom chased after her and shot her in the back twice. She then returned to finish off Freda with two more shots. Her glove was found near the bodies and it was thought that she had taken it off while reloading.

Back at the cottage the maid, Charlotte Saunders, was in the kitchen making tea. When Florence Ransom returned she tried to escape, but Ransom pursued her and finished her off. Six shots were fired in all, but the sound would have drawn little attention. At the time, Britain was expecting a Nazi invasion and Kent was full of soldiers in training.

Florence Ransom seemed unperturbed by what she had done. During her trial in November 1940, she underwent prolonged cross-examination without turning a hair. Throughout the procedure, she maintained that the whole day of the slaughter was a complete blank. However, she was identified by a porter at Tonbridge station and a taxi driver saw her taking the London train late in the afternoon. The jury took just 47 minutes to find her guilty.

'I an innocent,' she said, as the verdict was announced.

She then fainted in the arms of the wardresses and did not hear the death sentence being pronounced. Her appeal was turned down, though the defence maintained that the fact that epilepsy had impaired her mind had not been taken into account. At the hearing she could barely pronounce her own name and tottered from the dock, swaying and muttering. Later on, it turned out to be true that Mrs Ransom had a record of mental instability and was a voluntary patient on several occasions, so she escaped death by being sent to Broadmoor.

CHAPTER 27

VERA RENCZI

THE SEDUCTIVE BEAUTY Vera Renczi was the ultimate femme fatale. Sometimes called the 'black widow' because she always dressed in black, she killed two husbands, 32 lovers and her own ten-year-old son, keeping their bodies in zinc coffins in the cellar of her home so she could gloat over her handiwork.

Born in Bucharest, Romania, in 1903, Vera had a good education and was blessed with good looks. Her mother died when she was young and her father inherited some property in Berkerekul – now Zrenjanin – in Yugoslavia around 1916. She was a jealous child. When the dog her father had given her was found dead in the garden, Vera admitted she had poisoned it. Asked why, she said she had overheard him offering to give it to one of their neighbours because it barked too much at night, so she had decided that if she could not have the dog then no one else was going to have it.

Poisons first husband

Rebellious by nature, she was seldom without a boyfriend and when she had just turned 15 she was found at midnight in a dormitory of a nearby boys' school. Several times she ran off with her latest flame, only to return when she had tired of him. She then fell for a local businessman, many years her senior, named Karl Schick. He was wealthy as well as handsome. After a honeymoon in the Tyrol, they settled in a large mansion outside Berkerekul, where she played hostess to the notables of the city. After 14 months of marriage, she gave birth to a son they named Lorenzo.

Vera dedicated herself to being a good wife and mother but began to suspect that her husband was being unfaithful, so she poisoned him by putting arsenic in his dinner. She then told people he had gone away on business. Later she confided to friends that he had deserted her and had run off without even leaving a note. In fact, his body was lying in a zinc-lined coffin in the basement of the house. Meanwhile, she lavished all her attention on her son, who grew to resemble his father.

Second husband dies

After a year, Vera began to be seen out regularly in the company of young men. She then fell for a good-looking young scallywag named Josef Renczi and announced that she had just heard that her husband had been killed in a car accident. That enabled her to marry Renczi. Again she settled down as a dutiful wife, but her new husband also had a roving eye. While she realized that she could not monopolize the attentions of her husband, she would not endure another woman enjoying what she was denied. With the aid of arsenic he joined her first husband in the cellar, also in a zinc-lined coffin. Again, people were told that he had gone away on a long trip. Then after a year she said she had received a note saying that he would not be coming back.

Visitors never left

Despite her husband's philandering, Vera still maintained a lively interest in young men. She did not marry again but in the evenings she would haunt the cafés and nightspots of Berkerekul, seeking out male company. Known as the 'Mysterious Huntress', she would set her cap at strangers in town who would not be missed. She then took them home and after she had taken her pleasure with them they would not be seen again. It was supposed that they had gone back to wherever they hailed from, but in fact they had joined her husbands in the basement, each in a zinc-lined coffin.

It seems that Lorenzo then discovered his mother's secret. However, his silence was ensured by a dose of arsenic and he joined the others in a coffin in the cellar.

Tracked down by victim's wife

Vera's deadly game came to an end when she seduced a young banker named Leo Pachich, who had recently married. He was in love with his young wife, though, and when she fell pregnant he tried to break off his affair with Vera. She seemed to agree but persuaded him to stay for one last meal. It was indeed his last. His wine glass was laced with arsenic and strychnine.

When Pachich did not return from what was supposed to have been a short business trip, his wife contacted his bank. She was told that he had not been sent away on a business trip on the day he had gone missing – or at any of the other times he had been absent from home. She then went to the police, but as there was no suggestion of foul play they took little interest.

Mrs Pachich began making enquiries of her own. Those who knew her husband had little sympathy for a man who had abandoned his wife when she was expecting a child and she was told that he had been seen in a café in Berkerekul in the company of a beautiful blonde. When she informed the police, they had no doubt who the blonde was and at the wife's insistence they went to question Vera.

She admitted that Pachich had been her lover, but said he had not told her that he was married. When she discovered the truth, she said, she ended the affair and had not seen him since. The police accepted this story, but Mrs Pachich did not. She continued her enquiries and came up with a list of other men who had disappeared after being seen in Vera's company. Then she insisted that the police search Vera's house. Fearing that they had been bested in their investigations by a woman, the police surrounded the mansion and began a search.

Thirty-five coffins found

The cellar where the bodies were stashed was at the end of a long, vaulted stone corridor. To reach it, they had to break down three iron doors. But her servants were fiercely loyal and tried to resist the intruders. One old female retainer put up such a fight that the police were forced to handcuff her. When they eventually reached the huge, vaulted cellar, they found 35 zinc-lined coffins arranged around the walls, each one bearing the name of the occupant. They were all male. In the middle was a comfortable armchair.

Madame Renczi was then arrested in her well-appointed boudoir. When questioned by the examining magistrate, she denied everything and claimed that the bodies in the cellar were friends of her first husband, who had been killed by the Germans when they had raged through the Balkans in World War I. However, further investigation showed that some of the bodies belonged to men on Mrs Pachich's list. In a secret compartment behind a wall in Vera's boudoir the police found enough arsenic to kill 100 men. Arsenic was plentiful in Yugoslavia at the time – it was used in the production of alloys from the metal ores mined in the area.

Confession

The foreign press took an interest in what they called the Berkerekul Borgia. *American Weekly* of 22 August 1925 printed what purported to be her confession.

My first husband was the one who made me madly jealous of other women. I couldn't endure the idea of his ever looking at them! And after a year I felt that he would soon turn away from me, not entirely, but just enough to make me jealous. I swore to myself that he would never belong to another woman. So I killed him.

My second husband did not last as long. I was obliged to kill him after four months because he talked to other women. From that time on it became a disease with me. I wanted young men. Yet once I possessed them I could not bear the idea that any other woman might come after me.

I had the power to tantalize them. They would follow me. Then, perhaps a week after they had remained with me at my house, I would notice that they grew either distracted or would say something about having to return home. I would consider these first signs the beginning of the end. And, consequently, my first burst of passion for them would be followed by jealousy, and I would poison them without waiting any further.

No regret

Her motive was jealousy and she expressed no regret for the fate of her victims.

'They were men,' she said. 'I could not endure the thought that they would ever put their arms around another woman after they had embraced me.'

The examining magistrate asked: 'But why did you murder your own son?'

'He had threatened to expose me,' she explained. 'He was a man, too. Soon he would have held another woman in his arms.'

'And the easy chair in the cellar?'

'I liked to go down there in the evenings and sit among my victims, gloating over their fate,' she said.

Vera Renczi was sentenced to death, but this was automatically commuted to life imprisonment.

She died in a mental institution in 1939.

CHAPTER 28

TILLIE KLIMEK

ACCORDING TO THE *Chicago Daily Tribune*'s ace crime reporter Genevieve Forbes: 'Tillie Klimek went to the penitentiary because she had never gone to a beauty parlor.' Forbes pointed out that it was largely older, less attractive women who were convicted, while beautiful young women usually walked free. Following Klimek's conviction for murdering her husband in 1923, Forbes wrote:

> In recent years, the prosecution brought out, there have been 28 women acquitted of murder in Cook County. In most cases they have murdered their husbands. The only four women who have been convicted were:
>
> Mrs. Hilda Axlund, sentenced to 14 years for the murder of her husband. Mrs. Axlund was not a beauty.
>
> Mrs. Vera Trepannier, found guilty of manslaughter for shooting P.F. Volland, Chicago book publisher. Mrs. Trepannier was more than middle-aged.
>
> Mrs. Emma Simpson, found guilty of shooting her husband in a courtroom during a divorce trial. Mrs. Simpson was judged insane.

Mrs. Dora Waterman, convicted of murdering her husband, was sentenced to 17 years in the penitentiary. Mrs. Waterman was no beauty.

Mrs. Cora Isabell Orthwein, dashing well-dressed north-side beauty, is the latest woman to have been acquitted of murder. . . .

And Tillie Klimek, the squat, grewsomely [*sic*] cruel Polish woman, who rebuffs all human emotion from others, the woman who seems to take a grotesque delight in seeing others die, establishes the precedent in Cook County. Convicted of the murder of Frank Kupeczyk, she is sentenced to spend the rest of her natural life in the penitentiary.

In fact, she was lucky. While she was convicted of killing her third husband by putting arsenic in his food and the moonshine he drank, there was little doubt that she also murdered her first two husbands and tried to kill her fourth. But that was by no means the end of it. The police suspected she was responsible for the deaths of another seven people, while poisoning a further seven who survived. Assistant State Attorney William F. McLaughlin sought the death penalty, though no women had been executed in Illinois.

'Predicted' husbands' deaths

Born Ottilie Gburek in Poland in 1876, she emigrated to the United States with her parents at the age of one. They settled in 'Little Poland', on the north side of Chicago. The city had the second largest Polish population in the world after Warsaw at the time.

She married Joseph Mitkiewicz when she was just 14 in 1890. The marriage lasted all of 24 years, but in 1914 Tillie predicted that he would die within a few weeks. He fell ill and died on 13 January, as she had foreseen. The death certificate said the cause

Tillie Klimek was Chicago's so-called 'Lady Bluebeard' – she was sentenced to life imprisonment for the murder of her third husband.

of death was a heart attack and she collected a life insurance cheque for $1,000 (worth about £20,000/$26,000 in today's money).

She married again just after Valentine's Day. Tillie's second husband, John Ruskowski, died within three months, on 20 May, just as she had predicted, giving her something of a reputation as a psychic. He left $1,200 (£24,000/$31,000 today) in cash and $722 in life insurance (£16,000/$21,000), which she used to take her boyfriend, Joseph Guszkowski, on a romantic trip to Milwaukee. She was angling to make him husband number three, but when she let it slip that her first two husbands had not died of natural causes he got cold feet. Incensed, she threatened to have him prosecuted under the Mann Act, which made it a felony to transport a woman over a state line for immoral purposes. As it was, he went the way of her first two husbands anyway. All three men had died in a single year. Tillie bewailed her bad luck with men and cursed the ominous dreams that predicted their deaths.

'Only two inches to live'

In 1919, she married Frank Kupeczyk and moved to 924 North Winchester Avenue, now known on city guides as 'Old Lady Tillie Klimek's Haunted House'. The marriage was not a happy one and she took a lover. Then in 1921 she had another premonition, after which Frank fell ill. She told neighbours that he did not have long to live and then sat by his bedside sewing black lace on to the hat she would wear to the funeral. 'You'll be dying soon,' she told him. 'It won't be long now.'

Her landlady, Martha Wesolek, refused to let her store a coffin in the communal basement as Frank was not yet dead.

'I remember Mrs Kupeczyk came out in the yard with a piece of newspaper all about a fine coffin for $30 (roughly £350/$460 today) that she was going to get for Frank. I told her, "I chase you and the coffin out",' said Martha.

Tillie protested: 'My man, he's got only two inches to live.'

When Frank eventually lay dead in his bed, Tillie grabbed the corpse by the ears and shouted: 'You devil! Now you won't get up again!'

The death certificate said he died of bronchial pneumonia. Rather than being consumed with grief, Martha Wesolek recalled that Tillie played 'oh, so jolly music' on the Victrola.

She then bought the $30 coffin and wore the hat trimmed with black lace to the funeral. Frank's death netted her $675 (about £7,500/$9,900 now) in life insurance.

Husband survived rat poison

Fifty-year-old widower Joseph Klimek was in search of a new wife and attended the funeral, but Tillie did not stay around to flirt.

'She felt too bad to see people,' he said.

However, after a few weeks they did get together.

'I married Tillie for a home,' he said. He particularly liked her home cooking. Friends and family warned him that she was a woman with a past, but he wasn't worried.

'As soon as we were married,' he said, 'she burned up all the photographs of her husbands and her man friends. And she tore up all her letters. She had my picture over the mantel; that was all.'

But for her it was not a happy marriage. Tillie told her cousin Nellie Sturmer Koulik, who had also lost a husband, that it was not working out, but when Nellie suggested a divorce, Tillie said: 'No, I will get rid of him some other way.'

It seems that Nellie then gave her a tin of rat poison called 'Rough on Rats', whose active ingredient is arsenic. The brand's slogan was 'Don't die in the house'.

In September 1922 Joseph fell ill and Tillie predicted that he was going to die. However, his brother John suspected foul play as two of

Joseph's dogs had just died, so he called in the family doctor, Peter Burns. Joseph complained of agonizing stomach pains, his breath smelt of garlic and he had lost the ability to move his legs – all classic symptoms of arsenic poisoning. When he was rushed to Cook County Hospital, arsenic was found in his system, but after three months' recuperation he pulled through.

Bodies exhumed

On 26 October 1922, Tillie Klimek was arrested. As she was taken away, she said to Lieutenant Willard L. Malone, who led the investigation: 'The next one I want to cook a dinner for is you. You made all my trouble.'

Tillie was taken to the hospital to see her husband, who plied her with questions about his condition. She replied: 'I don't know. Don't bother me anymore.' When she overheard him asking for a glass of water, she shouted at the nurse: 'If he makes any trouble for you, take a two-by-four board and hit him over the head with it!' Nevertheless, to everyone's surprise, she kissed him before she left.

Tillie admitted feeding arsenic to Joseph Klimek, which she said her cousin had given to her, and the following day Nellie Koulik was arrested for providing the poison. The police then received an anonymous letter suggesting they look into the fate of Tillie's previous husbands. Frank Kupeczyk's body was exhumed and found to be full of arsenic, as were those of Joseph Mitkiewicz, John Ruskowski and Joseph Guszkowski.

Suspicious family deaths

In the same letter, Nellie Koulik was accused of being a poisoner, so the body of her first husband, Wojcik Sturmer, was also exhumed and was found to contain arsenic. At the time of his death she was having an affair with Albert Koulik, who became her third husband.

There were other suspicious deaths in the family. Sixteen-year-old Stanley Zakrzewski had died in 1912, 23-year-old Stelle Zakrzewski in 1913 and 15-year-old Helen Zakrzewski in 1915. They were cousins whose mother had fallen out with Tillie. All three had fallen ill after dining at Tillie's house and she had nursed them in their final illnesses. Again she had premonitions of their deaths, which she said were due to a deadly plague.

Nellie Koulik's infant daughter, Sophie Sturmer, died in 1917 and her twin brother Ben died a month later. Nellie's first husband had refused to acknowledge them as his. He died the following year, followed by Nellie's two-year-old granddaughter Dorothy Spera, who was in her grandmother's care at the time. A man named Meyers, thought to be another sweetheart of Tillie's, also went missing and two neighbours – Stelle Grantowski and Rose Splitt – reportedly died after eating sweets Tillie had given them following an argument.

Nellie's son John Sturmer fell ill after his father's death but recovered, though he remained convinced that his mother had tried to poison him. His sister, Lillian Sturmer, who lived with Tillie for about a year when she was 13, also fell ill. She too survived, but suffered from a heart condition for the rest of her life.

Cousin Nick Micko and Frank Klimek's sister-in-law Bessie Kupeczyk also sampled Tillie's cooking and fell ill. They lived, but a neighbour's dog whose barking Tillie found annoying was not so lucky.

Nellie's sister Cornelia was arrested when her son-in-law accused her of trying to poison him. The authorities talked of a 'poison ring' and called Tillie the 'high priestess of the Bluebeard clique'. Other local women were also apprehended in what Assistant State Attorney McLaughlin called 'the most astonishing wholesale poisoning plot ever uncovered'. However, they had to be released when no evidence for a conspiracy could be found. Nevertheless, the coroner declared: 'There is no question that Mrs Klimek poisoned everyone she wanted to get out of the way.'

Diagnosed as subnormal

In custody Tillie was cold and showed no emotion, while taunting Nellie that she was going to be hanged. Tillie protested her innocence, though to the press she was the 'Polish Borgia' and 'Mrs Bluebeard'.

'I didn't rob nobody!' she insisted. 'I didn't shoot nobody. I didn't poison nobody. I didn't kill nobody. I didn't! Everybody pick on me. Everybody make eyes at me like they going to eat me. Why do they make eyes at me? I tell the truth. Anything I did I did to myself. Nobody else.'

Genevieve Forbes was one of a group of feisty woman reporters on the case. She interviewed Joseph Klimek, tracked down Tillie's parents and then managed to interview Tillie herself, but she did not get much out of her. However, she was merciless in her description, saying Tillie was 'a fat, squat, Polish peasant woman, 45 years old but looking 55, with a lumpy figure, capacious hands and feet, and dull brown hair skinned back into a knot at the back of her head'. Nevertheless, she admired her self-possession, noting: 'Tillie Klimek is a spectator at her own drama . . . She has brains and they are the yardsticks for her emotions.'

Judge Marcus Kavanagh called for a 'psychopathic lab report' on the two women. The doctor who examined them concluded that they had a mental age of 11, though this could have been because they did not speak English well despite having been in the US since childhood. He concluded that they were both 'sub-normal mentally and sufferers from dementia praecox' – an old-fashioned term for schizophrenia.

Judge Kavanagh was also a devotee of eugenics. Noting that one of Nellie's sons had been diagnosed as 'feeble minded', he was convinced mental problems ran in the family.

'If we had a fieldworker, a eugenics expert, to check up on the history of this whole family at the time one moron was discovered,' he said, 'then the police might have been warned to watch this woman . . . when we find one case we can seek out and locate the nest.'

Tried for single murder

In the end Tillie only faced trial for the murder of Frank Kupeczyk. When the trial started on 27 February 1923, Joseph Klimek told the court that his food had tasted funny and that his wife had badgered him into taking out more life insurance. Other witnesses included neighbourhood gossips, a woman undertaker and three gravediggers. One related how Tillie's lover John would visit after Frank had gone to work.

'Once I seen him kiss her,' he said. When McLaughlin asked what happened next, the gravedigger answered: 'Why then, Tillie put up some newspapers in front of the window, so I couldn't see in.'

This provoked laughter in the courtroom, with Judge Kavanagh hammering his gavel and yelling: 'This is not a theatre!'

Appearing in the hat she had sewn beside Frank's deathbed, Tillie Klimek insisted that she had not murdered her husbands and that Frank had died of alcoholic poisoning. However, arsenic was found in all of their bodies.

'I loved them; they loved me,' she said. 'They just died same as other people. I am not responsible for that. I could no [sic] help if they wanted to die.'

McLaughlin told the jury: 'Gentlemen, the death penalty has never been inflicted upon a woman in this state. This defendant is like a good many other women in this town. She thinks she can get away with it. There are a lot of women, gentlemen, who are awaiting your verdict in this case. I feel that the death penalty should be inflicted, and I mean it.'

Tillie Klimek was found guilty of murdering Frank Kupeczyk, but was spared the gallows. Instead, she was sentenced to life imprisonment without parole, the harshest sentence ever given to a woman in Cook County.

Jailed 'because she was ugly'

Summing up, Judge Kavanagh said:

> This is one of the most remarkable cases in the history of criminology. The books do not contain another case like it. We have here a woman of average intelligence, a modern housewife and a good cook. When she is among women she is affectionate and, it is said, she is the most popular woman in the jail. Yet, the testimony showed, cold bloodedly, without feeling or remorse, she killed three of her husbands and attempted to kill a fourth.
>
> If this woman was let loose today, she would kill another man. She has a desire to see men with whom she was intimate suffer. Criminologists tell us there are a few such people on this earth. I venture to say there are more husbands poisoned in this community than the police or authorities realize. But the knowledge that Tillie Klimek has gone down will stay their hands.

He also ordered that she should not be allowed to cook while in prison.

Even though her children gave evidence against her, Nellie Koulik was thought to be simple-minded and was acquitted. The jury even found her not guilty of supplying Klimek with the rat poison she had used.

It was widely observed in the press that Tillie Klimek had gone to jail because she was ugly. A spoof telegram published in the *Tribune* read: 'Chicago's bid for fame in boosting Tillie Klimek will fall flat. Suggest you have eligibility classes as to beauty, social standing, and so forth before allowing any more murders.'

In a case sometime later, where two beautiful blond sisters were acquitted of murder, the prosecutor observed: 'Blond curls seem to have a faculty of making juries forget the most clinching evidence.'

As the sisters walked from the courthouse, someone in the crowd yelled: 'Remember Tillie Klimek.' This provoked laughter.

When Joseph Klimek died a few years later, the cause of death was initially given as tonsillitis. However, a post-mortem revealed that his body was still full of arsenic.

Tillie spent 13 years in the penitentiary, passing her time sewing. It was said that she enjoyed the prison food. She died in jail on 20 November 1936.

CHAPTER 29

JACQUI AND KELLY NOBLE

PERHAPS UNIQUE AMONG women who kill, Jacqui and Kelly Noble were a mother and daughter who were both convicted slayers, though their crimes were not related.

Abusive relationship

When Kelly Noble was born her parents, Jacqui Noble and Derek Benson, were both heroin addicts. Her childhood was also marred by violence because Benson regularly beat and abused Jacqui. Often seen in the accident and emergency department of the local hospital, she suffered extensive bruising and broken ribs. Once, when her brother-in-law stepped in to protect her, Benson threatened him with a knife. Jacqui obtained a banning order on Benson, but he simply ignored it.

Benson also abused Kelly, who came to the attention of Temple Street Children's Hospital in Dublin, Ireland when she was six. By nine, Kelly was fully immersed in the drug culture. Benson got her to sell fake drugs on the streets, putting her in harm's way so that he could get a fix, and she helped him inject. He also encouraged her to smoke marijuana.

According to Jacqui: 'He allowed her to drink alcohol and smoke hash and also showed her how to inject heroin. He had her going out selling "rips".'

There was little Jacqui could do to protect her daughter without risking a beating. She later told the court that Benson repeatedly raped her and that Kelly often witnessed this. He would also regularly terrorize the child in her bed, wielding a knife while wearing a balaclava.

In 1997, she secured another banning order on Benson, but again he breached it. When matters came to court, it was said that Benson tried to knock her down the stairs at a Garda station, after he was arrested for breaching the order. On another occasion, Benson hit her with a plank because she had failed to get up one morning and make his breakfast.

Arranges murder

Jacqui knew there was no escaping the abusive relationship. If she tried to leave, he would kill her, so she decided to strike first. She said that a man from Northern Ireland persuaded her that he could arrange to have Benson shot for £500 ($660), but he then disappeared with the money. Then there was a drug dealer, who promised to give Benson a 'bad dose of gear' in exchange for payment. This failed too.

She confided her plight to Paul Hopkins, the doorman at a local pub. He disliked Benson, who was always threatening to 'cut people up', and once, while he was away, Benson had threatened his girlfriend and their baby daughter.

Jacqui's mother then died, leaving her to care for her father, who was terminally ill. She seized the opportunity to leave Benson and move into her parents' home. But when her father died Benson also moved in, hoping to get a share of her inheritance. He took a bracelet her father had left her and demanded a cut when the house was sold. Instead, she offered Hopkins £3,000 ($3,950) to £5,000 ($6,600) from the sale, if he would dispose of Benson. She gave him a down payment of £200 ($260), though he said he would do it for nothing.

Hacked to death

Hopkins bought a sword from his brother for £50 ($66) and then gave Jacqui some sleeping tablets and a mobile phone. Benson was about to have some dental work done, so the plan was that when he returned from the dentist a little groggy, Jacqui was to feed him the sleeping tablets. When he was unconscious she was to phone Hopkins, who would come and finish him off.

Everything went according to plan. Hopkins turned up at the flat with the sword in a bag and asked Jacqui if she really wanted to go through with it.

'I was trying to get out of it,' he said. 'She said she was.'

Hopkins went into the bedroom when Benson was out cold and brought the sword down on the sleeping man. Then everything went wrong. Shocked by the sudden blow, Benson leapt up and a frenzied fight ensued. He suffered 25 serious stab wounds. The sword passed right through his body seven times and he was also partially decapitated. There were also over 60 defence wounds on his body, from when he tried to protect himself from his attacker.

The room was a wreck and spattered with blood. To conceal the evidence Hopkins decided to set fire to it, but a neighbour called the fire brigade, who put the fire out and found Benson's unburned body.

Life sentence

Jacqui Noble was an immediate suspect. As the long-suffering partner of an abusive man she had the motive for murder and she had just come into some money, so she also had the means. After a few days, Hopkins was brought in for questioning. The sword was found in the wardrobe of a friend's house.

'She said if I did it, she would pay me,' he said.

Both Paul Hopkins and Jacqui Noble were charged with murder. However, Jacqui was certain that she could beat the rap. She told friends that the last three women who had come before the courts accused of killing an abusive partner had walked free.

One friend said: 'I'm afraid Jacqui thought that because she had a violent partner it was a reason to kill him. There's a big difference between defending yourself from an attack and hiring someone to cut off someone's head. Jacqui was in a fantasy world and was convinced she would get away with it.'

Despite the murder charge, Jacqui was not held on remand. Instead, she and Kelly were rehoused in the coastal village of Laytown, 25 miles (40 km) north of Dublin. After years of abuse, Kelly had turned into an angry young woman. She also fell in love with an addict who had convictions for robbery, attempted robbery, arson and criminal damage. By the time she was 19, she was the mother of two. Soon she had no mother to help her, as Jacqui was convicted and began her life sentence.

Long-running feud

Kelly had a long-running feud with Emma McLoughlin, who was also a mother of two by the age of 19. The two had fought and Kelly had kicked her in the stomach while she was pregnant. On 2 June 2006, Kelly spent the afternoon plaiting her friend Niamh Cullen's hair as a birthday present. That evening, she strapped her young son Leon into his pushchair and went to Pat's Supermarket, 500 yards away, to buy some milk.

Emma was also in the supermarket, after spending all afternoon drinking with her sister and friends. She marched up to Kelly and demanded repeatedly: 'Why did you kick me in the stomach when I was pregnant?'

Emma suffered from ADHD (attention deficit hyperactivity disorder) and would not relent, even though two store workers tried to intervene. They noticed that Kelly's nose was bleeding and gave her a tissue. Emma was escorted to the door, but she would go no further and waited for Kelly to come out. Meanwhile, her younger sister Shona tried to calm her down.

Friend brings knife

Kelly told one of the shop assistants she would 'slice up' Emma. She then called Niamh and asked her to bring a knife. Niamh slipped an 8 in (20 cm) kitchen knife into an old school bag and brought it to her. She also had Kelly's daughter Jasmine with her.

'She asked me to bring a knife down to Pat's Supermarket and to come down and collect the children,' said Niamh. 'I grabbed a knife, put it into a small schoolbag and hurried down to the shop.'

When Kelly asked Niamh whether she had brought the knife with her, she pointed to the bag she was carrying. Kelly took the bag, hung it over the handles of Leon's pushchair and slipped the knife up her sleeve. As Kelly emerged from the shop, she and Emma began shouting at each other. Emma pinned Kelly against the shop window, the children began to cry and Niamh tried to calm them down.

Nineteen-year-old Deborah Cantwell, who was also there, said she heard Noble 'asking for a blade or something'. She was in a really bad mood. Indicating Emma, she said: 'I'm going to slice her up.'

Meanwhile, Emma taunted Noble, saying: 'Fight me. Now I'm not pregnant.'

Fatal wounds

Kelly had the knife behind her back and claimed that 'Emma went for me'. She heard Shona telling her sister that she had a knife and to get away.

'I said "Keep away from me",' said Kelly, 'but she just lunged at me and the knife stuck in her.'

Kelly insisted that she did not intend to kill Emma McLoughlin. Afraid that she would be severely beaten, she just wanted to scare her and make her run away. She told the Gardaí: 'It was self-defence, big time.'

Niamh also said that she had only handed the knife over to make Emma back off. She then heard a loud thump but did not see the knife go in. Shona said: 'I seen Emma get stabbed. I didn't see the knife. When she took it out it was full of blood and I knew she was after stabbing Emma.'

Emma collapsed. The knife had pierced her chest and lungs and punctured her heart. Kelly then grabbed Leon's pushchair and strode off, with Niamh and Jasmine following. Niamh looked back to see Emma lying on the pavement. She died at the roadside.

Emma's older sister Edel also recounted how she rang Kelly after the stabbing only to be told: 'She deserved it.' At first, Kelly told the police that Emma had the knife, but later admitted that she had called Niamh, asking her to bring it.

Convicted of manslaughter

Kelly Noble was charged with murder. During her trial, she cried a number of times, notably when CCTV footage showed images of her young son.

The McLoughlin family were upset that Emma had been portrayed as a violent, volatile young woman at the trial. Maurice Daly, the former school principal in Laytown, described how he had written to the board of management in 1998, warning them that pupils and staff were not safe when Emma was around. He was also anxious to point out that although the school had requested an assessment of Emma in

1996, when she was ten, it was not until three years later that she was diagnosed with attention deficit hyperactivity disorder.

Emma's sister, Shona, told the Gardaí how her sister had kicked her unconscious and broken her jaw in a fight over a mobile phone. The court also heard of Emma's numerous dealings with the Gardaí over the years, as well as allegations of an assault on a 12-year-old neighbour and a seven-year-old child. Outstanding charges against Emma were due to be heard the month after her death.

The jury found Kelly not guilty of murder, but she was convicted of manslaughter and sentenced to ten years' detention, with the last two years suspended by the Court of Appeal.

'If I could change going to the shop that night, believe me I would have changed it long ago,' she wrote to the McLoughlin family. 'I'm so sorry the way this has ended. I wish that night never happened . . . I have more than remorse. If I could turn back the clock, I wouldn't have gone to the shop.'

The McLoughlin family were too grief-stricken to accept her apology.

Kelly was reunited with her mother behind bars. A model prisoner, she served just four and a half years. Jacqui, too, was eventually released on parole.

CHAPTER 30

AMY ARCHER-GILLIGAN

AMY ARCHER-GILLIGAN WAS a widow in her 40s when she stood trial for murder in 1917. She then lived out her days in a hospital for the criminally insane. The case was unlikely material for comedy. However, New York playwright Joseph Kesselring remembered reading about it when he was a boy and 20 years later he went to Connecticut to examine newspaper accounts and records. The result was the play *Arsenic and Old Lace*, which opened on Broadway in 1941 and ran for three and a half years. Veteran movie director Frank Capra then turned the play into a classic movie of the same name, starring Cary Grant.

Mrs Archer-Gilligan was born Amy Duggan in Milton, Connecticut in 1868, the eighth of ten children. There was mental illness in the family because her brother John became an inmate of the Connecticut General Hospital for the Insane in 1902 and he was later joined by one of her sisters.

Care home opened

In 1897, Amy married James Archer and the couple had a baby daughter named Mary. Four years later, they moved to Newington,

Connecticut, to work as carers for elderly widower John Seymour, in exchange for room and board. When Seymour died in 1904, the Archers rented the house from his heirs and turned it into Sister Amy's Nursing Home for the Elderly.

Seymour's family decided to sell the house in 1906 and the Archers moved on to Windsor, Connecticut, where they used their savings to buy a brick-built house at 37 Prospect Street. This became the Archer Home for Elderly and Indigent Persons. They advertised in local newspapers and handed out flyers to find clients, or 'inmates' as they called them. Lodgers could pay a weekly fee of $7 to $25, or a flat fee of $1,000 (worth over £18,000/$24,000 now) for lifetime care. Many chose the latter option.

As care for the elderly outside the family was relatively new, there was little regulation of care homes. However, in 1909 the McClintock family of West Hartford sued the Archers for their poor treatment of an elderly family member. The case was settled out of court, with the Archers paying $5,000.

Death of husbands

In 1910, James Archer died of Bright's disease, a catch-all name for kidney failure of an unknown cause, leaving Amy with a 12-year-old daughter to bring up, which was not cheap. Mary had been enrolled in Windsor's Campbell School for Girls, where the fees were $410 a year (about £8,500/$11,000 now), plus $50 for piano lessons, as she was a budding musician. Amy also found herself liable for back taxes and wrote to Windsor tax collector Howard L. Goslee, saying:

> I ask to be dealt with honestly – that is all – I fully realize
> my great loss and sorrow and that I am alone dependent
> upon myself to care and educate my little daughter who was

deprived of her dear father whom she loved so dearly. But I am not afraid to demand justice, and I think it is about time that it is shown me.

In 1913, Mrs Archer married again. Her new husband was 56-year-old Michael Gilligan, but the marriage lasted just three months, as Gilligan suddenly died.

The death certificate listed 'valvular heart disease' as the primary cause of death, with a secondary cause given as 'acute bilious attack' – that is, very bad indigestion. He left her $4,000.

Flat fee residents died soonest

While many of the inmates of the Archer Home could not be expected to live long, 61-year-old Franklin R. Andrews was surprisingly fit and healthy. He did gardening and work around the house and ran errands for Mrs Archer-Gilligan. Andrews often wrote to his sister, Nellie Pierce, mentioning the frequent deaths at the care home. The mortality rate was particularly high among those who paid the flat fee. Those who paid weekly could expect to live longer.

On the morning of 29 May 1914 Mr Andrews was seen painting a fence on the property, but at 11 o'clock that night Mrs Archer-Gilligan phoned his sister, telling her that he was ill. However, she said it would not be necessary to visit until the following morning. When Mr Andrews' sister arrived the next day, she was told that her brother had died in the night. The cause of death was given as gastric ulcers. His sister grew suspicious about his death when she went through her dead brother's papers and discovered that Mrs Archer-Gilligan had been badgering him for money. She went to the district attorney, who showed no interest, so she approached the local newspaper, *The Hartford Courant*.

High mortality rate

The *Courant*'s correspondent in Windsor, Carlan Goslee, wrote the obituaries of the town's residents and had long been troubled by the death rate at the Archer Home. He visited the local drugstore, H.H. Mason's on Broad Street Green, and examined the poisons register that every drugstore was obliged to keep. There he discovered that Mrs Archer-Gilligan often bought arsenic, saying she used it to kill rats and bedbugs.

Courant editor Clifford Sherman then opened a full investigation. Reporters went through the death certificates and found there had been 60 deaths in the Archer Home between 1907 and 1916 – 12 before 1911 and 48 from 1911 to 1916, after Mrs Archer-Gilligan had got into financial difficulties. This was a shockingly high mortality rate, as only ten or 12 people lived at the home at any one time. The Jefferson Street Home in nearby Hartford had a similar number of deaths but had seven times as many inmates.

Residents at the Archer Home frequently died suddenly and the death certificate often cited a stomach problem. It was then discovered that just before Michael Gilligan's death Mrs Archer-Gilligan had bought 10 oz (283 g) of arsenic – enough to kill 100 people. Reporters also found that she had been buying morphine.

The state police then began to take an interest. On 2 May 1916, Mr Andrews' body was exhumed and his stomach was found to contain enough arsenic 'to kill half-a-dozen strong men'. This led to other bodies being dug up too – including that of Mr Gilligan.

Money taken from deceased

A week later, the state police went to the Archer Home to ask Mrs Archer-Gilligan about the deaths of her inmates. She said: 'Well, we didn't ask them to come here but we do the best we can for them.

They are old people, and some live for a long time while others die after being here a short time.'

Questioned about the financial arrangements she made with the deceased, she said she barely scraped by: 'I am a poor, hard-working woman and I can't understand why I am persecuted as I have been during the last few years. This is a Christian work and one that is very trying as we have to put up with lots of things on account of the peculiarities of the old people.'

On 8 May 1917 she was arrested for murder. She protested, saying: 'I will prove my innocence, if it takes my last mill. I am not guilty and I will hang before they prove it.'

The following day, the front page of the *Hartford Courant* carried the headline: 'POLICE BELIEVE ARCHER HOME FOR AGED A MURDER FACTORY.'

The story under it read:

The arrest of the Windsor woman yesterday is the result of the suspicions aroused when Mrs Nellie E. Pierce of No. 205 Vine St., Hartford, found in the effects of her brother, Franklin R. Andrews, after he died at the Archer House, a letter from Mrs Archer-Gilligan asking for a loan, 'as near $1,000 as possible,' about which the woman had said nothing to her.

When Mrs Pierce asked Mrs Archer-Gilligan about the loan, she denied receiving one at first. Later, she said she had received $500 as a gift. After Mrs Pierce had hired a lawyer to demand the return of the money, Archer-Gilligan paid it back, 'not because she could not keep it but because she did not feel it worth quarreling over,' the *Courant* reported.

Statement of the accused

From Hartford County Jail, Archer-Gilligan issued a long statement, saying:

> Shortly after Mr Andrews's death, I received information that the authorities were trying to connect his death with some criminal act on the part of somebody in the home. Some of the neighbours in Windsor distorted the facts and invented stories to keep the agitation alive.
>
> Some of the inmates of the home told me from time to time that they were told they were liable to be poisoned if they remained in the home, and one old gentleman, over 90 years of age and ailing, went so far as to intimate that a glass of lemonade served to him when he was suffering from a severe cold had been drugged. The physician in attendance on him at the time was requested to make an analysis of the lemonade and did so by drinking it in the presence of the old gentleman who suspected it was drugged. The man still lives.
>
> For a period of several months I was constantly informed that the authorities had examined the conduct of the home, but, knowing that I had done no wrong and that there was nothing that I should fear as a result of the investigation, I continued to manage the home and solicited patronage.
>
> Many of the inmates die, which is not strange, because they were sent to the Home when they were either too old or too feeble to care for themselves and at a time when their relatives considered them such a burden that they had to be cared for by some institution. Most of them were ailing from diseases other than those which usually accompany advanced age. In each instance, when a death occurred the relatives were notified, unless, perchance, the relatives had

left word not to be notified, in other words, had abandoned the inmate.

I have had hundreds of aged, helpless and infirm and have ministered to their wants and given them such comforts as the Home could afford, and I think they were all satisfied with the treatment received. When I was arrested, I asked the police officers if it would not be better for me to consult an attorney, and they told me to follow their advice, that they were friendly to me and wanted to carry the thing through without notoriety. I followed their advice, and now I am in jail without a hearing.

The public knows nothing of my side of the case, nothing about the real facts behind my arrest and imprisonment. After I was locked up here in jail Captain Hurley of the State Police came to me, again advised me as a friend, and told me that they had four charges of murder against me. If I was to sign a statement, he said, admitting one charge, they would drop the other three. Thank God I did not follow his advice because my counsel informs me that if I had this so-called friend would have rounded out his friendly advice with a conviction on the awful crime of murder, and I am innocent of wrongdoing against any person who had ever been an inmate of my house, in either thought, word, or deed, as any child of 5 years.

I am told it is claimed that I took persons under a life contract and tried to make a profit by poisoning them. An examination of the records, which have been seized by the State Police, will show the absurdity of such a statement. I have conducted this home for years. I inherited a little property from my parents, and when my husband, Mr Gilligan, died he left a will, leaving his property to someone other than myself. I am today in jail, charged with murder, knowing nothing of the evidence against me nor whom it is that I am charged with having murdered.

I have two small pieces of real estate, worth from $8,000 to $9,000, mortgaged for $4,750, and I have worked all my life, cooking and scrubbing and washing, giving personal attention to the home and trying to educate my 18-year-old daughter, who is heartbroken because of the charge which has been brought against me.

When she was here at the jail this morning it almost broke my heart to learn that a picture of my baby had been put on the front page of a Hartford newspaper. This was a cowardly outrage, and I hope the man responsible for it will some day feel a little anguish and agony which a mother's heart feels now as a result of his mean and contemptible conduct.

When I was managing the home I contracted small bills, and my lawyer tells me today that a kind-hearted Deputy Sheriff in Windsor has placed attachments upon the little bit of property I had, making it impossible for me to further mortgage and so raise funds for my defense. It seems as if all the world has turned against me, and at times I feel a forlorn and defenseless woman, but I try to have faith in God, and my love for my baby girl will give me strength to live until my innocence is proved. I want a chance to prove my innocence.

This statement was reprinted in *The New York Times* under the headline: 'MRS. GILLIGAN SAYS SHE IS PERSECUTED.'

Arsenic found in corpses

The newspaper went on to report that the State Bacteriologist, Dr A.J. Wolff, said enough poison had been found in Mr Andrews' body to kill several people. The embalmer, Frank P. Smith of Hartford, said he did not know if arsenic had been used in the preparation of the embalming fluid.

'The fluid came from New York,' he said. 'I don't know the formula.'

Another of the bodies to be exhumed was that of Mrs Alice Gowdy, who had died at the age of 69. She and her 71-year-old husband, Loren B. Gowdy, had enquired about moving into the Archer Home in May 1914. They wanted to move into the room occupied by Mr Andrews on 1 June and he died conveniently on 30 May. The Gowdys got a telegram the following day, saying they could move in after they had stumped up the fixed fee of $1,000. Mrs Gowdy died on 4 December 1914 and when her body was exhumed it showed traces of arsenic. However, Mr Gowdy survived long enough to testify at Archer-Gilligan's trial over two years later.

Life sentence

While the authorities thought Mrs Archer-Gilligan had killed at least 20 residents, she was indicted for the murders of five people: Franklin Andrews, Alice Gowdy, Michael Gilligan, Charles A. Smith who died on 9 April 1914 and Maud Howard Lynch who died on 2 February 1916. All but Lynch had died of arsenic poisoning – she had been poisoned with strychnine. However, Mrs Archer-Gilligan was eventually tried for only one murder, that of Mr Andrews.

The trial began on 21 June 1917 in Hartford. It drew large crowds and was covered widely in the press. Mrs Archer-Gilligan was convicted and sentenced to death by hanging, but the conviction was overturned on a technicality and a retrial was ordered. At the second trial in June 1919 she changed her plea to not guilty on the grounds of insanity. A forensic psychiatrist then confirmed she was crazy, while her daughter Mary testified that her mother was a morphine addict. The trial ended abruptly when Mrs Archer-Gilligan changed her plea again, this time to guilty of second-degree murder. This brought a life sentence.

Arsenic and Old Lace

She began her sentence at the state prison in Wethersfield, but five years later she was certified insane and transferred to the Connecticut General Hospital for the Insane at Middletown. There she was described as a quiet and co-operative patient. When she died in 1962 at the age of 94, the *Courant* reported: 'Mostly she sat in a chair, dressed in a black dress trimmed with lace, a Bible on her lap, and prayed.'

In the play and film *Arsenic and Old Lace*, the 'Connecticut Borgia' was transformed into two sisters, maiden aunts living in Brooklyn. Their victims were aged men who lived in their boarding house and the old-fashioned murder weapon of choice was elderberry wine spiked with arsenic. The cast of characters included a dotty brother, Teddy – who thought he was Teddy Roosevelt at San Juan Hill and was forever yelling 'CHARGE!' and running up the stairs – and two nephews, the sane Mortimer and the homicidal Jonathan.

The Duggan family continued to live in the village of Milton in Connecticut. One of Amy's brothers would stand in front of a mirror all day, playing the violin. He shared a house on Saw Mill Road with a sister who became an invalid after jumping or falling from a second-floor window.

Doubts about guilt

There are some who doubt that Amy Archer-Gilligan was guilty. The Windsor Historical Society maintains a file on Amy Archer-Gilligan and when Ruth Bonito from the Historical Society of nearby Windsor Locks checked it out she concluded that Amy may have been innocent. She never confessed to the crimes and the evidence against her was purely circumstantial. Although she bought arsenic, she may well have used it to kill rats and bedbugs, as she said. The Archer Home did have a high mortality rate, but that did not prove that she poisoned the inmates – or that they were poisoned at all.

True, arsenic was found in the bodies that had been exhumed. However, arsenic was once used extensively by American embalmers, a fact confirmed in 1997 by Connecticut's state archaeologist, Nicholas Bellantoni. In 1908, Connecticut's legislature banned embalming fluids containing arsenic because its use made it impossible for forensic scientists to ascertain whether residues in bodies were the result of poisoning or embalming. Formaldehyde-based embalming fluids were to be used instead, but these gave off toxic fumes and could only be used in places where there was proper ventilation. Consequently, some undertakers continued using arsenic-based fluids illegally. At the very least, this could have been a key argument for the defence.

Mrs Bonito also pointed out that Amy Archer-Gilligan was a churchgoing woman who donated a stained-glass window to St Gabriel's Church in Windsor. This hardly made her the type of woman who would turn to serial killing in middle age.

CHAPTER 31

TRACEY CONNELLY

IN NOVEMBER 2008, the mother of Baby P, Tracey Connelly, pleaded guilty to causing or allowing the death of her 17-month-old son Peter, who had suffered more than 50 injuries over the previous eight months, including a broken back. The child's identity was suppressed at the time as Connelly and her boyfriend faced further criminal charges. If she were identified, it could prejudice a future trial.

Taken into care

Born on 29 June 1981 in Leicester, England, the result of a liaison between a travelling salesman and her Irish-born mother Mary O'Connor, Connelly was brought up with her brother, who was four years older than her. She was 18 months old when she was taken to London by her mother, who regularly smoked cannabis and struggled with alcoholism. At 12, she discovered that the man she took to be her father, Garry Cox, was not her biological parent.

'It sent me a bit wild for a while,' she said. 'I went through a period of wanting to find him.'

She eventually made contact with her real dad two years before Baby P died. Giving evidence at her trial, he said her home was a 'revolting pit'.

A troubled child, Connelly claimed she was physically abused and was taken under the wing of Islington social services, along with her sibling. She was given the choice of going to a children's home or a

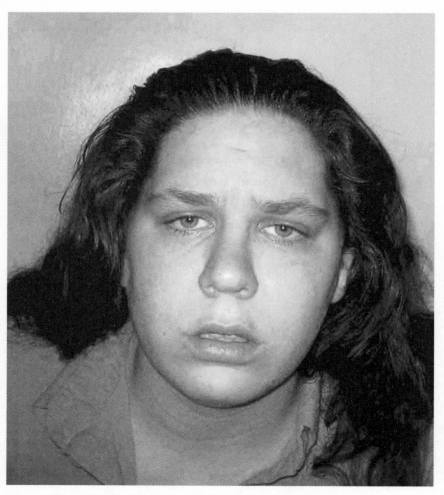

Tracey Connelly had a baby called Peter who had bruises on his head and chest. Connelly said he had fallen down the stairs.

special boarding school for delinquent children and chose the latter. Her sibling went to the children's home, where he was targeted by a paedophile ring. First he was a victim and then he was groomed to lure other children from Islington homes into the grip of the abusers. In a separate report, he became Child A.

Failed marriage

Connelly left school after three years with a handful of GCSEs, including English and IT. Though she never had a full-time job, she worked part-time as a hairdresser and in a bar. When she was 16, she met a 33-year-old London Underground driver.

They moved in together and had two daughters before they were married in a civil ceremony in 2003. The reception was held in a north London pub.

A year later she met Steven Barker, a part-time handyman who was working on a friend's home. Tall, blond and well-built, he was 12 years younger than her husband, had an IQ of 60 and was obsessed with the Nazis.

By then she had a third daughter and on 1 March 2006 Peter was born. She was said to have been delighted, but she soon fell into post-natal depression. At that point she began an affair with Barker. Her husband moved out in July after she took Barker with her to a school reunion and had his initials tattooed on her back.

First signs of child abuse

Barker then moved in with her, but she hid his presence from the authorities in case she lost the £450 ($590) a month she received in benefits or the allowance paid by her estranged husband. But all was not well with baby Peter. In October 2006 his GP noticed bruises on his head and chest. Connelly said that he had fallen down the stairs. In December, he had more injuries to his head and chest, along with the bridge of his nose, his right shoulder and his buttocks. The GP referred him to Whittington Hospital. Less than satisfied by Connelly's explanation, the paediatrician there called social services.

Peter went into care over Christmas. Away from his mother he did well and put on weight, but he showed signs of being disturbed, headbutting and biting his carer. Meanwhile, the police visited Connelly's home. They found no visible signs of injury on Peter's sisters, but the place was a mess. So social services provided the family with a new four-bedroom council house in Tottenham, unaware that Barker was going to live there too.

Filth and neglect

'My life is crazy,' she wrote on the social media website Bebo. 'Have moved house and I'm loving my new place. My fella is nuts but being in love is great.'

Then in June 2007, Barker's coercive older brother Jason Owen moved in with his 15-year-old girlfriend, five children, a dog and a pet snake. Connelly asked Owen to leave and when he refused she grew depressed.

'I'm fed up with letting people down,' she wrote on a website. 'All my life I have messed up. When will I ever get it right? People should stay away from me as I have always messed up everyone who's close to me. I'm a jinx to all I know.' Another post read simply: 'Life is bullshit.'

Connelly spent hours on her computer or watching American crime dramas such as *CSI*, while drinking and smoking. Otherwise she lay on the sofa, trawling pornographic websites or playing online poker. Peter would be left lying in his cot without being fed properly or having his nappy changed. The house also showed signs of neglect. There were faeces, both animal and human, on the floor and the dismembered corpse of a rabbit lay on the kitchen table. The place was infested with fleas and there was a layer of filth on every surface. Connelly then had Peter's head shaved. She said this was to rid him of head lice, but the numerous cuts on his scalp became infected.

Doctor misses serious injuries

Other signs were missed by social workers and medical staff, who saw Peter more than 50 times in his short life. He was on the child protection register and was visited twice a week by health or social workers, but Connelly told them lies and smeared the child with chocolate to hide his bruises. She was arrested for suspected child cruelty on 11 December 2006 and 1 June 2007, after referrals from social services. However, the Crown Prosecution Service said: 'Due to the conflicting nature of the evidence received after the second arrest, the CPS had no choice but to conclude that there was no realistic prospect of a conviction.'

This continued right up to Peter's death. Shockingly, Dr Sabah Al-Zayyat saw Baby P at a child development clinic at St Ann's Hospital in Tottenham, north London, on 1 August 2007, but missed his injuries after deciding she could not carry out a full check-up because he was 'miserable and cranky'. Two days later, Peter was found dead in a blood-spattered cot. A post-mortem examination found he had probably suffered the most serious injuries, including a broken back and fractured ribs, before he was examined by Dr Al-Zayyat, who became suicidal after the child's death. There were 22 injuries on his body. A fingernail and a toenail were missing, ripped out in some form of torture, his earlobe was torn and his spine had been fractured by being bent over the edge of his cot or someone's knee. Clearly the little boy had been the subject of sadistic abuse.

Interview with social services

Four months before Peter died, his mother had an hour-long interview with Sue Gilmore, the senior team manager overseeing the case. In it, Tracey Connelly talked about her friend Steven.

'He is 6ft 4in (193 cm), blond hair, green eyes and I am sorry if I've built up a dreamboat on him, but he is every girl's dream,' she said.

Asked about her son's injuries, Connelly said: 'We are at a friend's house. Peter fell and banged his chin and he got cut there and there and [there was] a graze when he caught himself on the table. But my instant reaction well after initially petting him was to take photos of the table so that I can show the social services, well, I think it's what happened. Because I was scared that if there was no evidence they were going to say that I done it.'

She also made it clear that she wanted to be left alone by social workers.

'I don't like having people interfere,' she said. 'I don't mean that in a horrible way. I know that the social worker is there for a job, and I know they are there for a purpose, and at the end of all this I hope they will back off and leave me alone so that I am a caring mother. Does that make sense?'

'That's a fairly straightforward thing to want,' said Gilmore. At the end of the interview, she thanked Connelly for being 'really open, completely honest', adding: 'I'm impressed, really, really impressed.'

Death of Baby P

On 3 August 2007, an ambulance was called to Connelly's house. The crew had been told that a child had stopped breathing. They found the toddler in a filthy bedroom. He was dressed only in a nappy and was already blue and stiff to the touch. Attempts to resuscitate him failed and the paramedics told Connelly that they were going to take him to North Middlesex Hospital. She asked them to wait while she got her cigarettes.

Further efforts to revive him met with no success and the police were called. Connelly was arrested and then taken to Edmonton Police Station. Officers went around to the house where they found Barker, who said he was just visiting. It was only after he was formally arrested that he admitted having a sexual relationship with Connelly. Indeed, he was the father of the child she was expecting – she was three months pregnant at the time. Owen was arrested too.

Peter's bedding was missing and an attempt had been made to cover up what had happened to the child. However, as it was not clear who had inflicted the final act of cruelty that robbed Baby P of his life, a charge of murder could not stand. Instead, those who had been arrested were accused of 'causing or allowing the death of the child'. Connelly pleaded guilty, while Barker and Owen denied any involvement. They were convicted.

Indeterminate sentence

Barker and Connelly were also charged with the rape of a two-year-old girl. Barker was convicted, while Connelly was cleared of causing or allowing the abuse of the girl. Before sentencing, Connelly wrote to the judge, saying: 'I except [*sic*] I failed my son Peter for which I have pleaded guilty. By not being fully open with the social workers I stopped them from being able to do a full job, as a direct result of this my son got hurt and sadly lost his short life.'

It did no good. Judge Stephen Kramer called her 'selfish, calculating and manipulative' and said that her insistence that she was unaware of what was going on in the house and what suffering Peter was enduring at the hands of Barker and his abusive brother Owen 'defies belief'. During the trial, she had shown little emotion, let alone contrition. Labelled a risk to children, she was given an indeterminate sentence and ordered to serve a minimum of five years. She gave birth to her fifth child in Holloway Prison and the infant was taken into care.

Barker was given 12 years for causing the death of Peter and life for the rape of the little girl. Owen was also given an indeterminate sentence for causing Peter's death. On appeal that was reduced to six years.

Oblivious to crimes

On the day she was sentenced, Connelly said: 'Every day of my life is full of guilt and trying to come to terms with my failure as a mother. I punish myself on a daily basis and there is not a day that goes by where I don't cry at some point.'

This may have been disingenuous. She seemingly remained oblivious to her crimes. A month after sentencing, she wrote to a friend: 'I have never been the best mum in the world but I'm not the worst and I'm not the sort of mum who would hurt her children.'

She continued to blame Barker and deny that she knew what he was doing.

'As the weeks and months passed I slowly started to wake up to the truth,' she said, 'so now I hope he rots in hell.'

Sometimes she could be more self-pitying, saying: 'I trusted Barker so much, we got together (he is five years older than me) then bang, him and Owen did what they did and now I'm here!! . . . I'm a good person who got stuck in a f****d up situation.'

Too obese to climb stairs

Nevertheless, she was already planning to have a good time once she got out of prison, writing to a friend: 'I tell ya, when I get out. I'm in no rush to get in a relationship with a man again, but I might have fun playing the field and travelling (one long party!). Hope you're going to join in the party.'

In another letter, she wrote: 'I would love to visit Egypt and Greece and Rome. I would love to see the pyramids and go down the Nile.'

Already overweight, in prison Connelly piled on the pounds, watching TV and stuffing herself with chocolate. Once she was publicly named she had to be segregated from other prisoners and so joined Rosemary West in Low Newton, near Durham. In prison, she also hooked up with Toni Hewitson, a lesbian who had been jailed for sexually torturing a woman with learning difficulties.

When Connelly was moved prior to release, the two women exchanged letters in which they made plans to get together again on the outside. They intended to live together. Connelly was released on licence in November 2013 but was returned to jail after breaking her parole conditions by selling nude pictures of herself online.

In 2018, she was given a cell on the ground floor at Low Newton, because she had grown too obese to get upstairs.

'She's too fat to tackle the stairs, so she's been moved downstairs,' reported the *Daily Mirror*. 'She can hardly walk a few yards without getting out of breath. She spends all her cash in her prison account on chocolate and crisps. She is a giant slob who spends most of her days eating.'

The newspaper also reported that she had requested a hysterectomy as she did not want any more children. She could not trust herself with their safety on the outside. However, at 29 stone (184 kg), she was judged too heavy for surgery.

INDEX

PICTURE CREDITS